ANDERSON, Thomas C. The foundation and structure of Sartrean ethics. Regents Press of Kansas, 1979. 184p bibl index 79-11762. 14.00 ISBN 0-7006-0191-0. C.I.P.

A thorough examination of Sartre's normative thought. Anderson attempts to show that there is a coherent and consistent ethical structure which runs through both the earlier and later writings of Sartre by manifesting how the concept of freedom elucidated in the existential works is completed by the social and political structures urged in Sartre's more recent Marxist writings. Anderson brings in the works of Simone de Beauvoir to clarify and expand Sartre's arguments where they are sketchy. The views of Sartre's critics on ethics are carefully reviewed and often shown to lack a full understanding of Sartre's enterprise. Anderson presents his own helpful criticisms of Sartre's arguments and position. In general, the book offers a lucid and scholarly construction of Sartre's ethical theory and a lively discourse concerning its adequacy. It is an excellent reference work for both undergraduate and graduate libraries.

The Foundation and Structure of
SARTREAN ETHICS

The Foundation and Structure of
SARTREAN ETHICS

Thomas C. Anderson

THE REGENTS PRESS OF KANSAS
Lawrence

© 1979 by The Regents Press of Kansas
Printed in the United States of America

Library of Congress Cataloging in Publication Data

Anderson, Thomas C   1935-
The foundation and structure of Sartrean ethics.
Bibliography: p.
Includes index.
1. Sartre, Jean Paul, 1905-   —Ethics.
2. Ethics. 3. Liberty. I. Title.
B2430.S34A75   170   79-11762
ISBN 0-7006-0191-0

Contents

Preface

This book is the result of my frustration in searching for suitable materials to use in teaching university courses in ethical theory over a number of years. Though any teacher of such courses has at his disposal numerous anthologies and surveys that appear to set forth every ethical theory under the sun, from deontological to utilitarian, from Platonic to emotive, there are none that adequately present the views of existentialism, even though this philosophical movement has been from its beginning vitally concerned both theoretically and practically with moral issues. This omission seems particularly unfortunate and unnecessary when it comes to the ethical views of Jean-Paul Sartre, who with Simone de Beauvoir is the last of the living originators of existentialism.

To be sure, most ethics books and anthologies do mention Sartre and some of his moral positions; how could they ignore a man who time and again has publicly taken moral stands, often of a very controversial nature? But the presentation is usually superficial and incomplete, if not downright erroneous, leaving one with the impression that Sartre has either said next to nothing about moral theory—or that nothing he has said is philosophically intelligible—both of which impressions are false. It was out of a desire to remedy this situation that I undertook research into Sartrean ethics and the writing of this book.

It is not generally appreciated that the foundations as well as the broad outline and structure of this ethics were set forth by Sartre and de Beauvoir in their early works, mostly written during the 1940s, and they have given no indication that their moral position has changed in its essentials since that time. Except for one significant area, human relationships, the ontology on which this moral theory is based is that expounded by Sartre in his monumental work of that period, *Being and Nothingness*. In this book I present that early ethical theory and show how it rests on that ontology.

To do this a detailed discussion is necessary of some of those ontological positions, namely, the ones which furnish the underpinnings of the morality. In the course of this exposition I indicate the shifts that have occurred since *Being and Nothingness* and that have some bearing on the ethics. I have not found it necessary, however, to delve into the more general issue of the overall development of Sartre's thought. Even to trace its evolution from its dualistic form in his early work to its dialectical form in the *Critique of Dialectical Reason* would demand a study much larger than this one and would take us far beyond our topic. Thus, I do not go into the question of whether his *Critique* is consistent with the positions of *Being and Nothingness*. (I attempt to show, however, that Sartre's analysis of human relations in the *Critique* is compatible with his ethical theory and, in fact, to some extent serves to flesh out its moral ideal.) There is no doubt that a general investigation of the progression of Sartre's thought from *The Transcendence of the Ego* to *L'Idiot de la Famille* would be immensely valuable, and I hope to contribute to it at some future time. In this present book I have set for myself the more modest task of expounding the first principles and general structure of Sartrean ethics and those ontological positions which supply their proximate bases. I hope at least to explode the myth that this ethics is nonexistent and/or radically unintelligible.

I would like to acknowledge the assistance of many

persons in the preparation of this book, particularly my colleagues at Marquette University, who have been a constant source of stimulation. I especially wish to recognize the assistance of Patrick Coffey, Howard Kainz, and Walter Stohrer, for helping me formulate my thoughts and words. Two former students, Linda Hansen and Stephen Dinan, have also contributed immeasurably to this endeavor. I want to thank the Marquette Committee on Research for financial aid in the preparation of this manuscript, and Carol Worm and Barbara Olson for their labors in this regard. Finally, my deepest gratitude to my wife, Kathryn, whose editorial advice was invaluable and whose encouragement was unceasing.

The Foundation and Structure of
SARTREAN ETHICS

Everything that I have tried to write or do in my life was meant to stress the importance of freedom.

—Jean-Paul Sartre, 1975

1

The Present State
of Sartrean Ethics

A. Introduction

"If God is dead, everything is permitted." The ethical thought of Jean-Paul Sartre is a response to this challenge from Dostoevsky, a challenge to construct a viable moral position in the face of the death of God and the absence of any objective moral values. The universe in which Sartrean morality must find its home is a sterile one, devoid of all intrinsic value and meaning, a universe with no inherent justification for being. It is a world in which God—or any transcendent source of meaning, whatever it is called, and hence any *a priori* objectively given realm of values—is totally absent. It is a world, in short, in which man must create whatever sense and worth there is. Can man live meaningfully in an intrinsically meaningless universe? Can any ethical values to assist him in so doing be constructed in an objectively valueless world? This is precisely the challenge Dostoevsky stated so well, and it is the purpose of this book to show how Sartre meets it. In general this investigation of Sartrean ethics will be most instructive for anyone who questions whether ethics can make sense, whether in fact it can exist at all, in the absence of objective values.

Needless to say, Sartre believes it can, and we will see to what extent his view is justified.

However, to speak as I have of Sartrean morality or ethics (I use the terms interchangeably) is sure to invite objections from those familiar with the works of this prodigious author. The fact is that he has never published a work on ethics. For over thirty years now, philosophical as well as nonphilosophical readers have waited for the work Sartre promised in 1943 on the last page of *Being and Nothingness*. Thousands of pages of this ethics were written, and as late as 1969 it seemed that publication would soon be forthcoming. Yet to date the work has not appeared; and now, since Sartre has practically ceased writing, due to near blindness, it apparently will never reach print—at least not in his lifetime.[1] Its absence no doubt explains why in spite of the continued interest in Sartre's thought in the 1970s, as shown by the publication of numerous books and articles devoted to it, few of these publications have much of anything to offer when it comes to explaining his ethical positions.

Many commentators on Sartre's thought have failed to realize that Sartre himself, in various places in his early writings, has indicated the foundation and the general structure of his ethics. Moreover, the works on ethics of those closest to him—namely, Simone de Beauvoir and Francis Jeanson—can offer invaluable assistance in determining the character of his ethics. De Beauvoir's *The Ethics of Ambiguity* is said, by the author herself, to be based on the ontology Sartre expounded in *Being and Nothingness*.[2] Furthermore, Sartre's glowing letter-preface to Jeanson's *Le Problème Moral et la Pensée de Sartre* leaves no doubt that the book has his imprimatur and that it can be considered to accurately present his own thought. I have no hesitation, therefore, in using these works as authorities in the following chapters, though the major focus of my attention remains, of course, the published work of Sartre. Wherever possible, I have let Sartre speak for himself. I have taken pains to use his own words to document the positions I set forth as his, especially in those instances that might be controversial or where I disagree with standard interpretations.

My version of Sartrean ethics is, in fact, frequently at variance with the views of many of his critics who, I believe, have often badly misunderstood Sartre's position. I sometimes think that few philosophers of our century have had their views so regularly distorted and misrepresented as has he. This erroneous understanding is in no little way due to a superficial reading of his works, a superficiality evidenced by the failure of some critics to provide anything close to adequate textual support for their interpretations. This is perhaps forgivable when Sartre's philosophy is approached by nonphilosophers from the perspective of his literary and dramatic works. But it is inexcusable when philosophers, who should have the patience and skill to grapple directly with the intricacies and obscurities of his technical philosophical writings, are guilty of the same misrepresentations. In many cases a close reading of his own words will destroy these erroneous interpretations—though it certainly will not remove all problems. This book is not the first attempt to set the record straight; but, to my knowledge, it is the first in English to be devoted exclusively to explaining his ethical thought by means of thorough textual analysis. I might add that my analysis also reveals that Sartrean ethics possesses definite similarities to traditional moral theories.

The major portion of my book, then, presents the foundation and general structure of Sartrean ethics based on Sartre's own works, supplemented by those of de Beauvoir, in particular, and of Jeanson. My approach is as objective and sympathetic as possible, for I consider this ethics to be one of the most coherent attempts to respond to Dostoevsky's challenge. Still, though Sartrean ethics has much to recommend it, I believe that in the final analysis it contains serious difficulties which must be examined—in many cases, though, not the difficulties others claim to find. Each chapter, in fact, includes a critical evaluation of the doctrines set forth in it.

The remainder of this introductory chapter, section B, is devoted to explaining why Sartre's own work on ethics has never appeared in print. It seems appropriate to cover this here since so many commentators have maintained that internal difficulties within Sartre's philosophy have prevented the appearance of his ethics. They have claimed that the ontological positions of *Being and Nothingness* have undermined its possibility. For example, some say that his views of the nature of value, human freedom, and human relations make it impossible for Sartre to propose any meaningful statements about how men should and should not act toward each other—and at the very least, I presume, any ethics has to include such statements. Others argue that Sartre's denial of all objective values makes him unable to designate consistently some conduct as morally good, some as morally bad. In much the same vein other critics (the most notable among them Mary Warnock), while granting that there are ethical dimensions to Sartre's later thought, maintain that this is possible only because he no longer accepts much of his earlier ontology. They insist that it is only because of a radical change on his part, a "radical conversion" from existentialism to Marxism, that a Sartrean ethics becomes possible. All these critics agree that if he adheres to the ontology of *Being and Nothingness* Sartre cannot propose a viable ethics, that only by repudiating this ontology and embracing another can he find the proper foundation for morality.

In the chapters to come, and especially in chapter 2, I deal extensively with the objections briefly sketched above, showing that a great number of them are rooted in misunderstandings of Sartre's ontology. This is not to deny that some of his early positions appear to present serious difficulties for an ethics; it is to claim that once the ontology is understood correctly, many, though not all, of these difficulties can be resolved. I believe it is more accurate to say that on balance Sartre's early ontology is not so much an obstacle to the development of his ethics as it is its very foundation. Even his present espousal of Marxism does not involve wholesale rejection of his existentialism. There is no doubt that his thought has developed over the thirty years since he wrote *Being and Nothingness*. His ontology has been modified in a number of areas. However, neither he nor de Beauvoir has given any indication that his moral positions have changed in essentials over that period. The ethical theory, which was set forth primarily in works written in the 1940s, remains for the most part founded on the early ontology. Only in the area of interpersonal relations were there changes which significantly affected his morality. Even here, Sartre merely supplied at a later date a more solid analysis of human relations, thus accounting for the ethical positions he had already adopted in some early works.

In subsequent chapters I examine the ontological views that form the proximate bases of Sartre's ethics, and I reply then to the objections briefly set forth above. In the remainder of this chapter I review the various reasons he himself has given for not publishing his ethics. To do this I have made extensive use of the recently published, excellent bibliography by Contat and Rybalka. While I am not personally satisfied that any or all of these stated reasons fully account for this lacuna in his writings, they do supply some explanation. Perhaps what is most significant is that nowhere in his writings does Sartre suggest that his ontology made the formulation of an ethics impossible.

B. The Unpublished Ethics

It would perhaps be helpful to realize from the beginning that the unpublished ethics is far from the only work that Sartre has promised but not delivered. Also missing are the fourth volume of *Roads to Freedom*, the second volume of the *Critique of Dialectical Reason*, and the last volume of *L'Idiot de la Famille*, as well as concluding volumes of his autobiography and books promised on Mallarmé and Tintoretto. For good or for ill, Sartre is clearly not the kind of author who confines himself to completing one work before beginning another. This can be explained partly by his statement in a 1960 interview that he has "always produced to order." "I have always produced a literature of occasional

7

writings," he explained, which seemed to be "ordered" by the particular situation in which he found himself at the time—for example, "a particular event that calls for comment."[3] It would appear, then, that a general reason the ethics promised in 1943 has not been finished and published is that events since then have made it less necessary in his eyes than the other works he has published. As the times have changed, what needed to be said changed.

Accordingly, it is easy to understand why Sartre has not finished or published his ethics since 1968. The events of that year in France caused him to significantly rethink his role as an intellectual in society. (I am referring to the revolt of many French students and workers and their occupation of schools and factories.) The radical change that took place in his conception of his intellectual role has been discussed by him in various interviews, one of the most important being in 1971 in the *New York Times Magazine*.[4] In it he reviews his life and work since 1940 and explains that from 1940 to 1968 he was only a "left-wing" intellectual. But since the events of 1968 he has become a "leftist" intellectual. The difference, he says, lies in action. No longer can the intellectual serve the oppressed masses simply from his office or study. He must join with them bodily in demonstrations, hunger strikes, counterviolence against police violence, occupations of buildings, staging people's trials, writing and distributing revolutionary papers, to list some of the things Sartre himself has been involved in. The intellectual must, he now believes, put himself *directly* at the service of the oppressed. His task is not to decide where battles are to be fought but to join physically with the masses wherever and whenever they battle, to join them in their strikes, in their occupation of factories, schools, and mines, and in their other specific actions against the system. He should not speak or think for the masses by devising theories that he expects them to implement. Rather, he must place his talent directly at their disposal by becoming their mouthpiece, expressing their specific grievances, their claims, and their goals in the concrete circumstances of their lives. This does not mean that the intellectual simply supports everything that the masses think, say, and do. He has a special role in sharpening their awareness and clarifying their needs and aspirations, and he must be willing to criticize them if they deviate from their principles.[5] Still, his place is at their side, fighting their fight. In this connection Sartre is reported to have said recently, "the only viable activity for the intellectual today is the political tract"![6] While I doubt that one can take this purported statement totally at face value, it serves to show the direction of his thought since 1968. The most profound intellectual analysis of contemporary men and society is no substitute for the actual liberation of men, Sartre now believes.[7] Clearly, spending time on a theoretical work dealing with the foundations and justification of an ethics would be rather difficult to reconcile with this extremely practical orientation. This in no way means that Sartre now considers morality to be worthless. Quite the opposite is true. He affirms his agreement with French Maoists inasmuch as they recognize that morality is concretely a fundamental force moving people to act. The drive for moral values—the love of justice and the hatred of injustice, for example—is the real impulse behind action. But he sharply distinguishes this "living" morality from present systems of morality, which he contemptuously dismisses as simply superstructures of capitalistic society and dead theories.[8]

Though this may explain why the ethics has not come into print since 1968, what about the twenty-five years between 1968 and 1943, years before Sartre became a "leftist" intellectual? Why was his ethics, a great deal of which (around two thousand pages) was apparently written during this time, never completed and published? There are apparently two major reasons. One is that most of this writing was lost.[9] Another, equally important, is that the ethics composed during the early part of this period was one he eventually came to reject. One of the criticisms he later leveled against it was that it was too individualistic. At the time it was written he believed that morality was primarily a personal matter. He did not sufficiently realize the engaged character of each individual, particularly his situation in society. Nor did he see that a morally good life in any full sense was impossible without a radical restructuring of the social order. This ethics he came to designate pejoratively as "idealistic," and as "a writer's ethics." By calling it "idealistic," Sartre apparently means that it was too individualistic and also that it was overly abstract and impractical, too far removed from reality, for it was an ethics by and for those who moralize only from their office or study. In addition, by labeling it idealistic, he means it was ethics written by one who at the time believed that writing itself was of intrinsic value and that he had a "divine" commission to be a writer.[10] On this latter point Sartre, in a number of interviews and in his autobiography, has admitted that until he was in his forties he suffered from a "neurosis," a belief that his existence was fundamentally justified by writing. He considered literature to be his means of salvation, his religion.[11] In the early 1950s he concluded that the ethics he was writing while gripped by this "madness" was actually a form of escape from reality, an escape prompted "when technical and social conditions render positive forms of conduct impossible."[12] He came to realize that the ethics he was working on was so idealistic as to be impossible, for it presented moral good as if it were attainable without evil.[13] What was needed, he decided, was a relative and limited ethics proper to the human realm. In this realm good simply cannot be sought or attained without evil. In the real world, which he believes to be fundamentally and structurally unjust, acts of moral purity are impossible.

The impractical and overly abstract character of this early ethics was also discussed by Sartre in a very significant interview he gave in 1954 to a writer for a Dutch journal.[14] He stated there that he had originally conceived of his ethics as a general theory constructed parallel to his ontology. But later, he said, he considered that to be too abstract, and proposed instead to begin with concrete social problems that give priority to social and political commitment. After all, he continued, philosophy is not just a theory but a force acting amidst the realities of everyday life. What he now wants, he said, is an ethical theory that is at the same time a praxis. Clearly, in terms of this goal, any abstract theoretical treatment of the general foundations and justification of an ethics would be highly suspect.

Further reasons why such a theoretical ethics came to be unacceptable to Sartre even before 1968 can be found in his description in 1965 of the proper role of the intellectual. In a series of talks entitled "A Plea for Intellectuals" he stated that the function of the intellectual in relation to the masses should not be to offer them "ideology." What the masses need, rather, is "knowledge of the world in order to change it."[15] The intellectual should use his talents to help the proletariat achieve self-consciousness so that it can master itself and its society. Even though this is not identical to his post-1968 view of the function of the intellectual—for, as we have seen, he is now even more committed to direct action with the masses—it seems clear that even this pre-1968 view considered an abstract theoretical exposition of the foundations and justification of an ethics to be of questionable value. It is worth noting that the *Critique of Dialectical Reason*, perhaps his major work of this period from the mid 1950s to 1968, is an attempt to do exactly what he encourages the intellectual to do. The *Critique* tries to set forth the structures of society and the various collectivities within it in their dialectical interrelations and in their relations to matter, an understanding of which would enable man more fully to control them instead of being controlled by them. This is the type of work that Sartre himself in the aforementioned 1954 interview characterized as a theory that is at the same time a praxis.

It should also be noted that in this pre-1968 period, even after his rejection early in the 1950s of the idealistic writer's ethics he had been working on, he nevertheless continued to write an ethics, one free from the defects of the earlier one. Contat and Rybalka report that in 1964 and 1965 Sartre took up the task of drafting a new ethics, a "dialectical" one. They relate that Sartre told them in 1969

11

that this ethics "was entirely composed in his mind, and that the only remaining problems he foresaw were problems of writing it up."[16] The reason he had not already finished it was not because of any conceptual difficulties but because he wanted first to finish his study of Flaubert. Though he has published three volumes of this study, the latest in 1972, he apparently had serious reservations about writing this work after the revolts of 1968, to which we have already referred.[17] This is understandable if in fact he now believes that "the only viable activity for the intellectual today is the political tract." And in the light of such emphasis on the practical it is also not difficult to see why a work on ethical theory has never been finished. Add to this Sartre's deteriorating eyesight, which he says makes reading and writing impossible, and the inescapable conclusion is that this work will forever remain unfinished.

Let me conclude this brief survey by reviewing the ground we have covered. From the forties until early in the fifties, Sartre worked on a general theoretical ethics parallel to his ontology, writing about two thousand pages on this topic. This was the ethics he apparently had in mind in 1943 when he promised at the end of *Being and Nothingness* to devote a future work to ethical questions. Much of this early work was lost; and, besides, in the early 1950s he came to reject this ethics as too idealistic and as a "writer's ethics." Nevertheless, he continued in the fifties to write occasional pages on moral problems. In the mid sixties he drafted a new work on ethics, a "dialectical" and practical ethics, and by 1969 it was entirely composed in his mind. This was set aside originally in order to complete his study of Flaubert. All of this is a matter of record, and most of it can be found in Contat and Rybalka's bibliography. My own addition to this story is the thesis that the events of 1968 turned Sartre so totally in the direction of practical writing of a social-political nature, as the mouthpiece of the oppressed in their concrete struggles, that this work on ethics has been relegated to the back shelf. Also, by 1975 failing eyesight precluded returning to it and finishing it, even if he wanted to.

I must confess that I am not satisfied that any of this adequately explains why Sartre, before the recent onset of near blindness, did not complete his ethics. It would seem that if he could justify his work on Flaubert after 1968 he could even more easily have justified finishing and publishing his work on morality. In any case the lacuna remains. I attempt with this book to fill it, at least in a general way. I do not propose to construct the "dialectic" ethics Sartre worked on in the sixties. Since he himself has decided that the pages of it that have been written will not be published in his lifetime,[18] and since I have no inside knowledge of its content, it would be ridiculous for me to attempt to reveal it. I have attempted, rather, to set forth the foundations and general structure of Sartrean ethics insofar as they can be gained from his scattered remarks in his published works, supplemented by the writings of de Beauvoir and Jeanson. As I have said, Sartre in various places, especially in his earlier works, has indicated the principles and general outline of his moral philosophy, and de Beauvoir's work is a particularly valuable supplement. I claim no more justification for my interpretations of his thought than I can textually support. Of course, Sartre himself in his present practical frame of mind might brand my endeavor here as idealistic (in the sense of overly abstract and impractical) and even "counterrevolutionary." Nevertheless, I would insist that what I am doing needs to be done. A thorough exposition of the foundations and justification of Sartrean ethics has simply not been written (or at least published) by Sartre, nor by anyone else. No one has undertaken the kind of careful textual analysis of Sartre's moral philosophy that I propose.

The exposition that follows presupposes on the reader's part a general familiarity with Sartre's ontology, especially as expounded in *Being and Nothingness*. In the following chapters I thoroughly explain only those ontological positions that are necessary for understanding the basis and general structure of his ethics. Any interested reader can find a

2
Preparing the Ground

Since critics have offered objections to a Sartrean ethics that,
if correct, would so undermine it that it could never get off
the ground, I believe it is necessary to begin by dealing with
these objections. This chapter, then, is devoted to respond-
ing to some of the most fundamental challenges to the very
possibility of an ethics based on Sartre's ontology. In the
process I set forth some of his ontological positions, a knowledge of which is necessary not only for grasping these objections and our responses, but also for understanding the
basis for this ethics.

A. Statement of the Objections

It has been claimed that Sartre's views of man, of God, and
of value render meaningless any ethical theory. One objection centers around his notion that man is a "useless passion." This "uselessness" is rooted in the fact that all of
man's passions, all of his desires, are for the same unattainable goal, to be God!

> Every human reality is a passion in that it projects
> losing itself so as to found being . . . which escapes con-

> tingency by being its own foundation, the *Ens causa
> sui,* which religions call God. . . . But the idea of God
> is contradictory and we lose ourselves in vain. Man is a
> useless passion.[1]

Since the goal of being God is unattainable, all attempts to
realize it, Sartre says, "are on principle doomed to failure.
Thus it amounts to the same thing whether one gets drunk
alone or is a leader of nations."[2]

One critic who sets forth the implications of this for
morality is Richard Bernstein. If man inevitably desires to
be God, if his life and actions all seek this impossible goal,
then "bad faith is the inescapable human condition," Bernstein claims.[3] He says this because he defines Sartrean bad
faith as the attempt by man to escape from what he is and to
become what he can never be. (Actually, Sartre's own definition is somewhat more complex, but that is not crucial
here.) The main point that Bernstein makes is that all man's
acts, even his so-called moral ones, are simply vain attempts
to escape from being man so as to attain the status of God.
But if bad faith in this sense is inevitable, any ethical theory
that would instruct men how they should and should not act
is meaningless. Indeed, one could wonder why he should
bother with morality at all since his absurd passion dooms
him to failure no matter how he lives.

In order to understand and respond to this objection it
is necessary to discuss at some length what Sartre means
when he says that all men desire to be God, an assertion
which on its face seems rather far-fetched. It is crucial here
to understand what he means by God. In many respects
Sartre's concept is a very traditional philosophical one. God
for him would be cause or foundation of himself (remember
the phrase *causa sui* in the passage documented by note 1
above). In addition God would be a necessary, not a contingent, being. That is, he would be a being whose existence
is not a mere matter of chance, but one whose nonexistence
is impossible. He would be *by right,* not by chance. God
would, thus, be a being who causes himself to necessarily

be, a being who necessarily is because of what he is, a being who could be said to have an *intrinsic* justification and right to exist. "But the idea of God is contradictory," Sartre claims. For if God causes himself to be, he cannot be necessary. In order to cause himself, God must first (ontologically if not temporally) be. Now, this God-as-causer, which pre-exists God-as-caused, would itself not be caused. As such it would be without foundation and so would be contingent, Sartre says: "In a word, God, if he exists [as a *causa sui*], is contingent."[4] Clearly, the idea of a being who is both contingent and necessary is contradictory. There is more to Sartre's notion of God, and more reasons why he considers this idea to be contradictory, but this will suffice for our purposes.

The question remains, why does Sartre believe that man desires to be this impossible being? As a first answer, let us point to some rather simple observations of a psychological nature that offer support to Sartre's view. Every man appears to have a fundamental desire to have a meaning for his life, a reason for being, a justification for his existence. Man can bear almost anything, even suffering and death, as long as he perceives meaning in it. Yet it is not just any old reason or meaning that will satisfy man. He rebels against considering his existence to be a mere accident or freak of nature, a mere chance occurrence that could have just as easily not happened. He will be content only with a reason or meaning that shows him to have a "right" to exist. He wants a reason for being, a meaning for his existence, that will assure him that it is necessary and not ultimately a purely unjustifiable, contingent event. In other words, man wants a reason removing his life from pure chance; only a reason giving him necessity will suffice.

No doubt some find such a reason and such a justification for their existence through faith in an omniscient and provident creator who gives each of his creatures an essential role in his Divine Plan. Sartre himself, in his autobiography, speaks wistfully of this faith he rejected years ago.[5] Other men, of course, seek to justify their existence through amassing wealth, or seeking fame, power, pleasure, virtue, knowledge, etc. "If I can just attain a certain income or a certain degree of power, or of fame, or virtue," a man says to himself naïvely, "then I'll have it made." He will have it made in that he will have attained such a status in reality that his life will be justified. He will have a *right* to be; his existence will no longer be a purely gratuitous accident of chance. Of course, in the final analysis no man ever has it made, but that is not the point here. Rather, the point is that men do seem to have a basic desire to justify their existence, to remove it from contingency, and do strive in various ways to do so. This is one dimension of what Sartre designates as the desire to be God.

There is another equally important dimension. Along with his desire for justification, man also desires to *give himself* this justification, Sartre claims. Because man is free he does not want his existence to be justified from outside of himself. He does not want to be simply a pawn in some cosmic Divine Plan, no matter how benevolent. Man wants the meaning of his existence under his control—if given freely from outside it remains contingent, and there is always the possibility that it may be withdrawn or that it may be imposed on him against his will. Of course, if the meaning of his existence comes necessarily from an external necessary being, then it is necessary, but he has no say in the matter. Since none of these alternatives is satisfactory, the only solution is for man himself to justify his own existence and give to himself a right to be. Are not the previous examples of man's seeking to attain meaning through fame, virtue, power, etc., all illustrations of his attempts to give himself, one way or another, such status in being that his existence would receive a necessary justification and right to be?

Now, for man to desire to be a being who would justify his own existence, a being whose existence is not by chance but who causes himself to be necessary, is precisely to desire to be God. As we said earlier, Sartre's concept of God is precisely that of a being who is *causa sui*, a being who necessarily is because of what he is, a being who has a right to be given to him by himself. Instead of being far-fetched, then, Sartre's assertion that man by nature desires to be God seems to be a very plausible, albeit rather dramatic, interpretation of man's most basic desires.

The preceding was primarily a psychological analysis. Actually, Sartre insists that his position here is not based upon an interpretation of man's desires and acts such as I have just suggested, but rather is founded securely on his analysis of the ontological structure of human reality.[6] Man is fundamentally different from what Sartre designates as being-in-itself, nonconscious beings which simply are what they are. A tree or a rock simply is what it is, totally one with itself. Man, however, is not simply one with himself, for he is always transcending whatever he is at a particular time and reaching for what he is not—a goal in the future. Inasmuch as man continually detaches himself from and transcends what-is, being-in-itself, Sartre says he is free from and lacks the simple self-identity of beings which are what they are. From his earliest philosophical work, *The Transcendence of the Ego*, Sartre has sharply distinguished between man and all other beings in this way. Man, or more precisely human consciousness, is nonsubstantial—that is, it is nothing but an egoless unity of intentional conscious acts whose being is totally in being related to its objects. Human consciousness is not contained in itself as things are; it lacks such self-contained self-identity by being totally in relation to its objects.[7] It is in this sense no thing, and Sartre even calls it nothing and nonbeing. Now, inasmuch as man is a lack of substantial self-identical being, man desires to be such a being, Sartre maintains. He desires to attain the oneness and solidity of being-in-itself. At the same time, man is structurally a radically contingent being, one which lacks a necessary foundation for his being. As such, he seeks to overcome this lack also. He is not satisfied with simply being; he wants to be "by right," by necessity. Man's goal, then, is to be a being who would combine both self-identity and necessary foundation. This would be a being who could not be derived from anything outside himself (else he would not be self-identical), but would have to somehow be necessarily founded by himself. We are, of course, describing the impossible *causa sui*, and it is precisely this that man desires to be because of his ontological structure.

To repeat the criticism given earlier: if man inevitably seeks to escape from being man to become God, what significance can any ethical theory possess? What is the point of attempting to say how men should and should not act if all his actions are necessarily directed to the attaining of that impossible goal? And if all are doomed to failure, what import is there to morality or to anything else, for that matter? So much, then, for this first objection. Later in this chapter I give Sartre's response.

Next, however, we turn to another criticism, one even more frequently voiced than the preceding, which also questions whether an ethics can be based on Sartre's ontology. This criticism, which includes many of the concepts just discussed (especially the idea of God as man's ultimate goal), centers around Sartre's notion of value. We met this objection briefly in chapter 1 where it was expressed in terms of Dostoevsky's challenge, "If God is dead, everything is permitted." Actually, the issue here is not so much atheism or theism but the presence or absence of objective values. Sartre's view, of course, is that it is man alone, more precisely individual freedom alone, that is the source of all values; no objective norms exist. He writes, "my freedom is the unique foundation of values and . . . *nothing*, absolutely nothing, justifies me in adopting this or that particular value, this or that particular scale of values."[8] He labels as cowards in bad faith those who hide this from themselves by accepting "the spirit of seriousness," the belief that values are objective realities built into things or acts independent of man's choices.[9] In this view man is free only in his response to these *a priori* existing values; he can accept or reject them. But even if he chooses to reject them, they remain values. Thus, for example, "seriousness" would claim that honesty or heroism would be of value whether or not anyone in fact viewed them as valuable, and even if all men denied they were valuable.

In opposition to this Sartre maintains that all values are due to man in his freedom.

Any number of critics have claimed that this subjectivistic position radically undermines the possibility of an ethics.[10] The English philosopher Mary Warnock, probably the best-known Sartrean commentator, makes this charge. She observes that in Sartre's ontology,

> We are debarred, on pain of Bad Faith, from asserting that anything is absolutely valuable. The particular kind of Bad Faith involved here is the "Spirit of Seriousness." The belief that some things are good in themselves, and the belief that some things are always good because their consequences are, absolutely, desirable are both equally expressions of this spirit.[11]

She goes on to claim that the moral norms that Sartre does propose are simply "incompatible" with this ontology and that it is difficult to see what significance ethics can have. Bernstein puts the objection even more strongly. He maintains that "if we hold fast to Sartre's ontological analysis, we can never justify any criteria, we can never ultimately say that one thing is more valuable than another." He, too, insists that Sartre's own moral statements, which approve some conduct and disapprove others, simply make no sense. In fact, he says, the logical consequences of Sartre's ontological position are "not only despair, but nihilism in the coldly technical sense"; for "there never is nor can be any basic reason or justification for one value . . . rather than another."[12]

It is not difficult to see what is at issue here and to sympathize with these criticisms. If no values are objective or intrinsically "built into" anything, if all values are simply created by each man himself, any ethics that would attempt to determine an objective set of norms stating what should or should not be valued by man is impossible. Are we not forced, then, to agree with Dostoevsky's challenge if rephrased this way, "if no objective values exist, everything is permitted"? Whether this is technically nihilism or not, it certainly seems to be the death of any ethics other than the most relativistic kind. At best, it would appear that Sartre can propose only a moral code (if it can be so dignified) in which each man should choose and do "his own thing."

Before I offer Sartre's response to this criticism, I think it would be well to take the time to explain exactly why he adopts a subjectivist position on value. In *Existentialism and Humanism* Sartre gives the nonexistence of God as the basic reason for his belief that no values exist apart from man's choice of them. There is no God to create or decree anything to be of value, and he even cites with approval Dostoevsky's words:

> The [atheistic] existentialist . . . finds it extremely embarrassing that God does not exist, for there disappears with Him all possibility of finding values in an intelligible heaven. . . . It is nowhere written that "the good" exists, that one must be honest or must not lie, since we are now upon the plane where there are only men. Dostoevsky once wrote "If God did not exist, everything would be permitted"; and that, for existentialism, is the starting point. Everything is indeed permitted if God does not exist. . . .[13]

In fact, it seems questionable whether atheism does necessarily entail a denial of all objective values. But that need not concern us here; for in *Being and Nothingness*, which contains a much more thorough discussion of the nature of value, atheism is never mentioned as the reason for Sartre's subjectivism. Rather, the latter is due to his conceptions of the nature of being as it exists in itself and of the nature of value. Sartre takes a back seat to no one in emphasizing the sharp distinction between facts and values. He explains that being as it is in itself simply is what it is. A tree is a tree, a historical or sociological fact is just that, a fact—something that is the case. But values, on the other hand, are ideals that lie beyond what is the case, ideals at present nonexistent which call for their realization. Sartre also calls values exigencies and appeals, which I experience as having some kind of a claim on me. They are experienced as demanding to be acted upon, demanding to be embodied in acts. Hence he also speaks of them in stronger terms as "imperatives," "tasks," "norms."[14] Certainly, what he is referring to here is common enough in human experience. In addition to experiencing what is the case, man experiences what is not but what appears to him as an appeal, an imperative that should be acted upon and realized in some way. To experience courage as a value is not for Sartre simply to perceive that courage exists as trees exist, but rather to recognize that courage should be embodied in acts in certain circumstances. Values are not existing facts that in themselves simply are and so can be noted by a disinterested spectator. Values call for, or even command, action; their very being is in being a demand for realization—and as something *to be made real* they must at present be "beyond being." They are something that is "lacked," Sartre says.

Another reason he refuses to consider a value as a being and a "fact among facts" is that if this is done "the contingency of being destroys value." The point is that values are not changed when their bearers change. Courage does not cease to be valuable because a courageous person turns coward and runs, nor because what is an act of courage in one circumstance becomes a foolhardy act in another. But if the value of courage were identified with its "concrete exemplifications" (Sartre's term), as concrete acts or persons ceased to be valuable, the value itself would be destroyed. Now, since values strictly speaking are not on the level of actually existing beings, since they are beyond what is, what reality they have can be due only to a being that is itself able to transcend what is and posit what is not. Such a being is, of course, human consciousness. Hence values are due to human consciousness.

However, values are due to human consciousness in quite different ways. Following Sartre, we must distinguish between the valuable goals that man seeks and the subsequent values that arise in terms of these goals. To illustrate the latter, if someone chooses as a goal a life of prosperity and comfort, material goods will have a great value for him. They will be experienced as things that should be sought. But for another person whose goal is an ascetic style of life, the same material goods will be practically insignificant in value. Of course, any particular goal would in turn have its value determined by more basic goals. And ultimately, Sartre states, each man's most fundamental goal, his fundamental project, will determine the value character for him of all his lesser goals and of all that is valued in the light of these goals.[15] But what about the fundamental project itself? From whence does it derive its value? Certainly not from some more fundamental goal. Rather, Sartre says, it is valuable simply because it is desired. In fact, we have already seen what in general man's fundamental goal, and hence his unconditioned value, is—to be God. Though he may attempt to attain this status in various ways (through money, power, virtue, etc.), being God is man's ultimate value. To speak of it as such is simply to mean that it is that lacked being that man ultimately desires. As we have seen, man desires and seeks it precisely because he lacks it. To be a man is to be lacking in and hence desirous of the necessity and self-identity of a self-cause. To be man, therefore, is to have God, in the sense of *causa sui*, as one's ultimate goal and value.

Now, according to Sartre, both types of value, the ultimate unconditioned one (being God), and the various relative ones which accrue to lesser goals and to things and acts because of man's goals, are due to man's freedom, though in quite different ways. Sartre himself, unfortunately, does not always keep these different ways distinct, nor do his commentators.

In the first place the relative values issue from man's freedom insofar as the goals he freely chooses inevitably give a certain value character to his subsidiary goals and to various beings in the world. If I choose to live a life of comfort in society, certain occupations as well as earthly goods take on a definite value for me. They have these values only because I choose the goal I do—thus I am the free source of their value. But the case is not the same as regards man's ultimate value or goal to be God. We have said that this is man's ultimate value precisely because he fundamentally lacks necessity and self-identity. We must now add that this lack of necessary self-identical being that is basic to man is equivalent in Sartre to human freedom—freedom not in the sense of freedom of choice, but freedom referring to the basic structure of man. For Sartre, the primary reason man is free is because he is ontologically not a self-identical, necessary being-in-itself. As a contingent being, he lacks and so is free from a necessary foundation. As nonsubstantial, he lacks the self-identity that chains things to being simply what they are and no more. Man continually transcends what is and what he is toward what is not. He is qua consciousness totally in relation to beings other than himself. This lack of self-contained necessary being is man's radical freedom, according to Sartre. He is free from the causally determined world of substantial beings-in-themselves precisely insofar as he is a lack of such being and continually transcends it.[16] We saw earlier that it is man's basic lack of self-identity and necessity that is the root of his desire to be God. Since this structural lack is also his ontological freedom, we can see why Sartre believes that it is man's freedom that is the root of his desire for God as his ultimate value.[17]

There is much that could be objected to in Sartre's analysis of the nature of human freedom, but this is a work on his ethics, not his ontology. For our purposes it is sufficient to note that this freedom, this lack of necessary substantial being, which is the basis of man's ultimate value, is not a freedom of choice. The relevant freedom here, man's structural freedom, is not one chosen by man but one which is present whether he likes it or not. And just as man does not choose to be structurally free, does not choose to be a contingent lack of necessary substantial being, so also he does not choose to desire to be this necessary self-identical being, God. It is no doubt true, and Sartre points it out, that individuals can freely choose various ways through which to try and become a necessary substantial being. As I have said, some men attempt to reach this impossible goal through wealth, some through power, others through virtue, etc. But

25

in each case the ultimate intelligibility of these various projects is the same. They are attempts to attain substantiality, self-justification, self-given necessity, the status of a *causa sui*. Clearly, then, this freedom, which is the source of man's ultimate value, is quite different from the freedom of choice, which is the root of all of man's other, lesser relative values.

It is time to state or restate the consequences of these notions of value for Sartrean ethics. Inasmuch as all values are rooted in man's freedom, none are objectively "in" acts or things. To say that something is valued is in the final analysis to say no more than that it is freely chosen to be of value; or, if the valued object in question is God, to say it is valued is to say that man inevitably desires it because he is structurally free. As the critics have pointed out, for Sartre any ethics that would attempt to determine an *objective* set of norms for man is impossible. Morality as a study of what values man *should* or *should not* choose seems meaningless. Whatever man chooses to value thereby has value. Furthermore, whatever a man does value, the fact remains that its value is only in relation to his ultimate value, which is to be God. And this position too, commentators maintain, renders ethics meaningless. If all man's values and all his acts ultimately are related to an impossible value-goal, one could reasonably ask why bother to be moral at all.

There are other positions in Sartre's ontology that critics have claimed make a Sartrean ethics meaningless, if not impossible, but they are not presented here. They are discussed at the appropriate place as I proceed in my analysis. The above objections were presented because they raise such fundamental challenges that they must be dealt with if one is even to begin to set forth the character of Sartrean ethics. In the next section of this chapter I begin to offer Sartre's response to these difficulties. His complete reply must wait, however, until chapter 3. Section B to follow centers primarily on Sartre's view that man by nature desires to be God, that being God is his ultimate value. Since this position is basic to both objections, a proper understanding and treat-

ment of it go a long way toward replying to and blunting
their force.

B. Sartre's Response to the Objections

As many have noted, from an ethical point of view the
most significant section in *Being and Nothingness* is the very
last one entitled "Ethical Implications." As its title indicates,
it deals with the ethical implications of the ontology and of
the existential psychoanalysis that Sartre has set forth in the
preceding pages of the book. Though some have found this
brief (three-page) section with its proposals for ethics highly
enigmatic, I believe that a careful analysis causes Sartre's
suggestions to emerge clearly.

Existential psychoanalysis should have as its principal
result, Sartre says, "to make us repudiate the *spirit of seriousness*."[18] As we saw earlier, this spirit involves the belief that
"values are transcendent givens independent of human subjectivity." In other words this spirit believes in objective
values. Sartre's existential psychoanalysis along with his ontology "must reveal to the moral agent that he is *the being
by whom values exist*."[19] Existential psychoanalysis should
also "reveal to man the real goal of his pursuit, which is
being as a synthetic fusion of the in-itself with the for-itself
[God]; existential psychoanalysis is going to acquaint man
with his passion."[20] Actually, Sartre goes on, many men have
in effect practiced this psychoanalysis on themselves and have
come to realize that their goal is to be God. Yet insofar as
they are still gripped by the spirit of seriousness and they
"still believe that their mission of effecting the existence of
the in-itself-for-itself is written in things, they are condemned
to despair; for they discover at the same time that all human
activities are equivalent . . . and that all are on principle
doomed to failure." Then follows the oft-quoted line, "Thus
it amounts to the same thing whether one gets drunk alone
or is a leader of nations."[21] Note particularly that this last
statement, as well as the mention of despair and failure, is

said with reference to those gripped by the spirit of seriousness. And in the passage this means those who believe that
being God has some objective value ("written in things").
The clear indication is that being God has no objective or
intrinsic value and that man is wrong to believe that it does.
Less obviously, Sartre may be saying that despair and failure
are inevitable only if one persists in taking God as his value
and vainly pursues this unattainable goal.

Sartre goes on: once ontology and existential psychoanalysis show man that he, as free, is "the unique source of
value," he will realize also that being God is simply one
value among others. And when this realization is joined with
the insight that the goal of being God is "doomed to failure,"
no matter how he tries to achieve it, man can consider, Sartre
suggests, the possibility that his freedom "turn its back upon
this value." Thus he states that freedom can "put an end to
the reign of this value [God]," and can instead "take itself
for a value" and "will itself freedom."[22] (What exactly "willing itself freedom" means is not spelled out but is left for
the future work on ethics.)

To sum this up, Sartre is claiming that it is not necessary
that man take God as the supreme value he will attempt to
realize in his life. Once ontology and existential psychoanalysis reveal to man that nothing, not even being God, has
any built-in or objective value, and also that to take God as
one's value dooms his life to failure, he can freely choose
freedom itself as his value. Note, by the way, that Sartre
never says that man can eradicate his *desire* to be God.
Rather, what he proposes is that once a man realizes the
vanity of this desire for an unattainable goal, he can take
some other end as his primary value.

There is, of course, one problem with these suggestions
which Sartre offers in his conclusion to *Being and Nothingness.* That is, earlier in that work, as we saw in section A,
he insisted that man cannot help but seek God as his ultimate
value. Indeed, in places he even goes so far as to say that man
must choose God as his ultimate value. Note these apparently unambiguous passages: "my freedom is a choice of be-

ing God and all my acts, all my projects translate this choice and reflect it in a thousand and one ways."[23] And in terms of value, "The fundamental value which presides over this project [i.e., man's fundamental project] is exactly the in-itself-for-itself. . . . It is this ideal which can be called God."[24] Finally, there is one very explicit passage: "if man on coming into the world is borne toward God as toward his limit, if he can choose only to be God, what becomes of freedom?"[25] Now, if he claims that man can choose as his ultimate value only to be God, how can Sartre in "Ethical Implications" suggest without contradiction that being God need not be taken as man's ultimate value?

One is tempted to say that in passages such as the above Sartre is guilty of extreme ambiguity if not equivocation in his use of the term "choice." To speak of man's fundamental desire to be God as a choice is certainly to use that term in a way radically different from normal usage. Ordinarily, choice implies the presence of alternatives. However, as we showed in section A, man, precisely insofar as he is a free contingent lack of being, necessarily desires to become a necessary substantial being who is cause of himself—God. No other alternative is possible, given what man is. The only sense in which man can "choose" to be God is the one also seen earlier. Man can choose the concrete way he will try to realize this goal, money, power, fame, virtue, etc. Nevertheless, and Sartre is perfectly clear on this, the ultimate meaning or intelligibility of any of these specific choices is to be God.[26] Each individual chooses his own unique way of being God, but a way of being God it is. That it is this is not chosen, at least not in the sense that any other alternatives are possible. This also means that man is not free whether or not to value this goal, which was discussed at length in section A. Insofar as man in his basic structure lacks the status of a necessary substantial self-cause, it is the ideal, the ultimate value, he desires. To call God a value here simply means that it is the lacked being man desires. He has no choice about this ultimate value since, again, no other alternatives are possible.

All this serves to sharpen the question posed above. If Sartre believes that man by his very ontological structure must seek God as his supreme value, even though he may choose various concrete modes of doing so, how can he in "Ethical Implications" speak of putting "an end to the reign of this value"? Sartre's answer, I believe, is found in a crucial distinction he makes in his discussion of value, a distinction between prereflective and reflective values.[27] After showing that man necessarily desires to be God and so designating God as man's ultimate and unconditional value, he goes on to point out that this value is often not explicitly known as such. Most of the time this value, like so many others, is simply lived nonreflectively as the lacked goal that man desires and seeks. Most of the time we simply take the values, the demands, we find in the world as given. We do not question their source or justification. Such "lived" values are distinguished by Sartre from those values that are grasped explicitly in an act of reflection. (These latter may be values actually conferred on reality by reflective consciousness.) Values on the lived, prereflective level, he explains, are present whether I am explicitly aware of them or not. For example, whether I know it or not, the lacked goal, and hence value, of my existence as a lack of necessary being is that being which would be a self-cause. But in reflection, Sartre says, I am free "to direct my attention on these [lived] values or to neglect them."[28] In other words, I am free in reflection to accept the lived values, or to neglect them and confer meaning and value on something else. By the way, this does not mean that these lived values are objective. The difference between them and values conferred by reflection is simply the difference between values that men make unknowingly and unreflectively and values men reflectively and knowingly produce. In fact, for Sartre one of the essential steps in breaking away from the spirit of seriousness and the bad faith that often accompanies it is to realize reflectively that I need not accept any of the values I find in my world as if they have some objective status.[29]

Though Sartre himself does not pursue this distinction

any further, the following application can be made. I do not by reflection have to reaffirm as valuable any lived values, and this includes both my desire to be God and its unattainable goal. Of course, this goal will still be valuable in the "lived" sense, meaning that it will still in fact be the goal of my fundamental desire. The crucial point to see is that it need not be a value that I deliberately choose to attempt to realize in my life. And I will see this, Sartre suggests, if I realize that the value of God is not an absolute intrinsic value but is one rooted in my very contingency. As we saw in section A, it is my freedom that is the source of the value in being God, freedom meaning my structure as a contingent lack of necessary self-identical being. Once I understand this —that is, once I realize that God is an ideal and value only in relation to a contingent being—I see that this value is only a relative one. It is not an absolute, not one which has *in itself* a right to be a value always and everywhere. Since all values are rooted in man, who is a nonnecessary being, "There is then a total contingency of being-for-value,"[30] Sartre says, and this contingency relativizes the value of being God, as well as all others. Once I realize the nonabsolute character of this lived value, I see at the same time that there is no necessity for me to choose to value it. I can "neglect" it and confer value on something else. While I will still fundamentally desire to be God, this goal will not be one that I will deliberately attempt to achieve in my life through my actions. (After all, desires do not have to issue into choices and actions.) This, I take it, is in essence exactly what he says in his conclusion to *Being and Nothingness*.

A question still remains, however, about Sartre's statements, cited earlier in this section, concerning man's necessary *choice* of God as his ultimate value. It is tempting to charge Sartre with equivocation in his use of the term "choice" here, but perhaps we need not go this far. It is worth noting that such statements occur late in *Being and Nothingness* in the section devoted to existential psychoanalysis, part 4 of the book. On the other hand, in part 2, in which he first discusses in detail his notion of value and explains his position that man desires to be God, he never refers to man's impetus toward God as a choice, nor does he state that man can choose whether or not being God will be his ultimate value. His emphasis is just the opposite, for he insists that because of his very structure man must seek to be God, and thus take God as his ultimate nonreflective or lived value. The reason why his later discussion in the section on existential psychoanalysis emphasizes man's choice in reference to being God is, I believe, that in this section he is primarily discussing not men insofar as they have a natural desire to be God but men who in fact do choose consciously and reflectively to value and strive to realize the impossible goal of being a *causa sui*. I say this because he states in an extremely significant (and almost universally ignored) paragraph in which he discusses play that *all* of his descriptions in the chapter, with the exception of that of play, are descriptions of projects undertaken by men who have not purified themselves from the spirit of seriousness, men who believe that being God has some objective value, which they, therefore, have to realize.[31] (In this connection it is worth noting that Sartre himself was later to characterize *Being and Nothingness* generally as a description of man in bad faith.)[32] Thus in this context Sartre's statements about men's choice to be God can be interpreted to refer not to all men but only to those who have taken God as their goal and value. Such an interpretation would, of course, square with his suggestions in "Ethical Implications." Still I would not deny that in assertions such as "he [man] can choose only to be God" and similar ones Sartre is guilty at the very least of being extremely unclear and misleading.

However one handles these particular statements of Sartre's in "Existential Psychoanalysis" so as to render them compatible with his suggestions in "Ethical Implications," I believe that his distinction between nonreflective and reflective values provides the basis for his reply to those who claim that he cannot consistently maintain that man is able to choose anything other than God as his ultimate value. Even though he desires—and so (nonreflectively) values—the ideal of being God, even though he can never eradicate this desire, man need not reflectively choose to value this unattainable goal. He is free to place his values elsewhere.

Not only is he free to place values elsewhere, he absolutely must do so, Sartre says, if he is to live a meaningful life. We have seen that for Sartre man's existence is useless and doomed to failure if he strives for the unattainable goal of being God. As an earlier objection stated, ethics itself is rendered meaningless if all of man's values and acts must be directed to attaining an impossible goal. But, of course, Sartre would say that this criticism fails to realize that man can refuse to value and to act for this end. If man in his freedom does reject this objective, if he chooses instead to value an attainable goal, then his existence is not at all meaningless or a useless failure. Likewise, contrary to the critics, ethics as a study of what values men should or should not choose and attempt to realize becomes extremely important. It is true that man does not intrinsically have a meaning or "use"; he is not by nature useful for some objective *a priori* value—for man alone causes all meaning and value. And this is precisely the significant point. The purpose, the "use," the meaning, of a man's life is exactly what he freely chooses it to be. Sartre explains: "to say that we invent values means neither more nor less than this; there is no sense in life *a priori*. Life is nothing until it is lived; but it is yours to make sense of, and the value of it is nothing else but the sense that you choose."[33] Man alone decides whether life is to be a useless failure or meaningful and useful. De Beauvoir puts this well when she says that for man to ask himself "whether his presence in the world is useful, whether life is worth the trouble of being lived" makes no sense.[34] It is up to man himself to give meaning and use to his life. He can do so by refusing to value his desire to be God and its impossible goal, and by instead choosing to value and seek goals that are attainable.

At the basis, then, of man's ability to create a meaningful human life is his freedom to refuse to value a goal he naturally desires and to create his own values. Now, recall that Sartre suggested in his conclusion to *Being and Nothingness* that man choose freedom itself as his ultimate value. The indication there was that, by so choosing, his existence would no longer be "doomed to failure" but would attain meaning and value. In fact, as we shall see, human freedom is the ultimate value in Sartrean ethics. In the next chapter I present Sartre's arguments in support of this, arguments which also serve to complete his response to the objections presented above in section A. The final section of this present chapter undertakes a critical review of the responses he has already offered.

C. Critical Evaluation

It seems to me that Sartre has done a good job in answering those who claim that his morality is pointless since human existence is doomed to failure inasmuch as man desires to be God. With his insistence that all values (including God) are rooted in human freedom, that none are objective or absolute, and with his distinction between reflectively chosen and lived values, he can legitimately argue that man need not choose being God as the value he will live for. It may be that man cannot help but desire that impossible goal; yet he need not choose to attempt to realize it.

This argument, in fact, is not an unusual one in contemporary ethical literature. It appears to be very similar to those advanced by critics of the so-called naturalistic fallacy, and it might be helpful to review it in this light. If we adopt Sartre's phenomenological description of value as that which men experience as an appeal, a demand to be realized, it seems perfectly consistent to characterize whatever men desire to attain as a value. Hence, men do in fact value happiness, health, pleasure, etc. But does the fact that man desires and therefore values such goals—even if it may be natural for him to do so—mean that he has to reflectively *choose* to value these desired goals, or values? It would seem not. Perhaps, as some anthropologists have suggested, men naturally desire to be aggressive. If so, aggression thereby becomes a value. But need it, indeed should it, be *chosen* as a value men should attempt to realize? The fact it is valued in the sense of desired by men—what Sartre calls a lived value—hardly demands that man must upon reflection choose to value it. Upon reflection a man might reasonably decide to attempt to ignore or at least frustrate this lived value. To argue that because man naturally *desires* certain goals, or values, he must *choose* them to be values that he will strive to realize is simply to be guilty of a *non sequitur*. Moreover, we have ample experience of situations in which we choose not to value the very goals (lived values) our desires impel us toward. Sartre seems to be on good grounds, then, in his distinction between nonreflective (lived) values, including some which man by nature seeks, and reflectively chosen values. He is also correct, I believe, in maintaining that once we realize that the former are not absolute values, that they have no intrinsic necessary right or claim to be values (not to mention that some are not even attainable), we can decide to neglect them and confer value on something else.

Following upon this, it is also legitimate for Sartre to maintain that human existence is not necessarily doomed to failure. Man can choose to value attainable goals, and in the realization of them his life will become meaningful—though why he proposes freedom as the primary goal remains to be seen.

There are two things that bother me, however, about Sartre's arguments. One has to do with his concept of the nature of value, the other with his claim that man naturally desires to be God. We saw above his understanding of value and his acceptance of a sharp fact/value distinction. Values are beyond being as ideals to be made real. They are not facts; they are not on the level of what is. This distinction is crucial to his argument. He can say that being God need not be chosen as a value, only because values are not objective or intrinsically part of any act or object. But this conception of value also has problems. For one thing, it seems questionable to claim that all values are nonreal and "beyond being." For another, even if one agrees with Sartre that values are not actually existent as facts are, this does not at the same time establish their nonobjectivity.

In the first place, we often use value terms to refer to presently existing acts or states. We say that this act of courage or state of peace is of value. Sartre, of course, admits this, yet claims that the values of courage and peace cannot be identified with their "concrete exemplifications." The values themselves are ideals to be made real, and as such cannot be concretely real without ceasing to be values. But this leads to very strange conclusions. Either values, precisely because by definition they are beyond being, cannot be instantiated (and then it is simply wrong for us ever to call an existing act or object valuable, and this clearly is not Sartre's view) or values can be present in some way in their concrete exemplifications. But if they can become actually present and so cease to be beyond being, values will thereby be destroyed as values, and Sartre says precisely this.[35] Indeed, just what it means for an ideal like courage to be concretely exemplified in courageous acts is itself left unanswered. (One is reminded of Plato's problems with the notion of participation.) There seems to be no way that Sartre's insistence on the nonbeing character of value can allow courage really to be in concrete courageous acts and hence permit men to speak of such acts as valuable. On the other hand, to claim that when a man calls this particular act of courage valuable it is actually some nonreality (ideal courage to be made real) that he is referring to, rather than this present act, seems ridiculous. Yet this is what Sartre's notion logically entails. What has gone wrong, I suggest, is that he has taken one perfectly legitimate meaning of the term "value"—namely, that which is a presently nonexisting ideal to be realized—and canonized it to the exclusion of all others.[36]

Furthermore, even if one accepts Sartre's arguments that values as such are distinct from their concrete embodiments, it is unclear why this must mean that they are nonobjective and created by man. It is interesting that in the section of *Being and Nothingness* that deals with value, Sartre cites the

German phenomenologist Max Scheler as one who correctly noted that values could be intuited in their concrete exemplifications and yet insisted on the distinction between values and their bearers. What Sartre does not say, however, is that though Scheler maintains the distinction between values and their concrete embodiments he in no way would agree that this means that values are nonobjective.[37] Sartre implies that to show that values are not concretely existing beings is to show that they are not objective but man-made. After arguing for the former position he immediately concludes, "These considerations suffice to make us admit that human reality is that by which value arrives in the world."[38] He appears to presume that to say values are not concrete beings is to say they are not beings *in themselves* at all. Since they obviously are present in human experience, if they are not beings in themselves, their reality must be due to man. But Scheler for one, G. E. Moore for another, and the whole Platonic tradition for a third would deny that to show that values are nonidentical with their bearers is to show that they are not beings in their own right. I am not trying to champion this view here. In fact, I find it difficult to understand what reality a value, or anything else for that matter, could have in itself apart from concrete acts and objects. All I want to suggest is that Sartre does not adequately show why maintaining that values are not concrete beings or facts means that they are not objective beings at all.

To sum up my criticism, it seems to me (1) that Sartre has rather arbitrarily adopted an overly narrow concept of value, and (2) that he has not adequately demonstrated his subjectivist position that all are man-made. It will be interesting to see, as we proceed with the elaboration of his ethical theory, whether he will be able to adhere to these views. Of course, whether or not he has adequately demonstrated his position, it will still be instructive to see how he can hold to a radical subjectivism about value and at the same time propose ethical norms (values) for all men to follow.

The other opinion of Sartre's that I wish to question here is his view that man necessarily desires to be God, *causa sui,* the foundation of the meaning of his existence. Let me state from the beginning that I do not consider Sartre's assertion to be foolish. Certainly, men do want meaning and justification for their lives. Throughout human history they have sought through religion, philosophy, science, art, etc., to attain a *raison d'être.*[39] Many, too, are not satisfied in obtaining this meaning from outside of themselves. They want to be in complete control of the sense of their existence. But that all men feel this way, that all basically desire to give meaning to themselves so as to preserve their freedom, is questionable. I see little evidence that many desire such radical personal freedom. Countless men appear quite willing to accept the meaning for their existence given by others, by gods or men, even by impersonal forces of nature. At the most they exercise their freedom only in accepting or rejecting that meaning from outside. In fact, many do not even admit to this much freedom, pretending rather that they have no choice but to accept the serious world. To insist, as Sartre does, that all men desire the freedom to create their own meaningful life, so as to be self-causes, seems simply contrary to the facts, especially to the fact that men more often join the crowd because they want to rather than because they have to. The additional fact that bad faith, in the sense of refusing to admit one's freedom, is so prevalent, according to Sartre, leads me to doubt whether man's desire to be the free foundation of his values is as fundamental as he believes it to be.

The preceding was a critique of the psychological side of Sartre's argument. His ontological demonstration, which he considers decisive, does not fare any better. Recall that this argument stated that inasmuch as man is intrinsically a lack of substantial self-identical being he desires to be such a being. Also, it was asserted that man as a radically contingent being lacking a necessary foundation desires to overcome this lack. The problem is that Sartre supposes that for man intrinsically to *lack* something means for him to *desire* that something. In *Being and Nothingness* he simply moves without explanation from one notion to the other.[40] I grant that man is intrinsically lacking in the substantial self-identity that things possess. But it hardly follows from this that he necessarily seeks such self-identity. This is simply another *non sequitur.* Actually, the man Sartre describes is the man who cannot rest content with being a creature. One is reminded of Nietzsche's statement, "if there were gods, how could I endure not to be a god!"[41] From the perspective of most religious traditions this man is the prideful individual *par excellence.* What Sartre fails to show is that all men in their heart of hearts really do want such a status in being. Perhaps in some deep, dark dimension of ourselves we do. I am not prepared categorically to reject Sartre's claim, yet, as I said, it appears to go counter to our all too observable willingness to deny our freedom. This position, that man desires to be God, has particular import in Sartre's view of human relations, as subsequent chapters demonstrate.

values men should seek and avoid. It would be wrong, however, to take this as implying a difference between moral and nonmoral values, for to my knowledge Sartre never makes such a distinction. It appears, rather, that he considers *all* values to be moral in character. Thus he frequently uses the terms "morality" and "ethics" to refer to any awareness or treatment of values.[4] If it seems strange to suggest that all values are moral in character, we should recall that for Sartre all values are ultimately connected to man's fundamental projects. And man's fundamental projects are certainly not morally indifferent inasmuch as they involve the basic way he relates to the world and to his fellow-man. Indeed, existential psychoanalysis, which attempts to reveal man's fundamental projects and values, is said by Sartre to be "moral description, for it reveals to us the ethical meaning of various human projects."[5] In context the "ethical meaning" of man's projects refers to the values toward which these projects tend. In any case, whether Sartre would accept a distinction between moral and nonmoral values or not, freedom is beyond doubt what Sartrean ethics takes as its fundamental value.

"Everything that I have tried to write or do in my life was meant to stress the importance of freedom," he has said in a recent interview.[6] The passages in "Ethical Implications," the last section of *Being and Nothingness*, which we analyzed in the previous chapter, leave no doubt that freedom is proposed in place of being God as man's primary value. Likewise in *Existentialism and Humanism* he states as a moral judgment that men should have as their ultimate goal "the quest of freedom itself as such."[7] Similar statements are made in *What Is Literature?*, "Materialism and Revolution," *Critique of Dialectical Reason*, and numerous interviews.[8] Simone de Beauvoir, throughout her *Ethics*, which as I noted she bases on the ontology of *Being and Nothingness*, takes freedom to be the supreme moral value. To cite just one text, "The man who seeks to justify his life must want freedom itself absolutely and above everything else."[9]

Perhaps one reason some have not clearly recognized that freedom is the ultimate Sartrean value is because in some of his works Sartre placed heavy emphasis on authenticity, as if it were primary. The most extended treatment of authenticity comes in his work *Anti-Semite and Jew*. There he says that authenticity "consists in having a true and lucid consciousness of the situation, in assuming the responsibilities and risks that it involves, in accepting it in pride or humiliation, sometimes in horror and hate."[10] In other words, the authentic person accepts himself in his situation as it truly is; he does not flee from it in self-delusion. He accepts the responsibilities and dangers that his situation involves, including, ultimately, responsibility for himself, for "he is what he makes himself" in and through his action upon the situation.[11] Sartre is not advocating here a passive acceptance of or acquiescence in the situation. In fact, for the Jew in an anti-Semitic society, he asserts that "authenticity manifests itself in revolt"[12] against the falseness of the prejudices and values accepted by anti-Semites in a spirit of seriousness and imposed on him. This revolt, he says, is ultimately for a society based upon real human equality and solidarity, a society, in other words, based upon the true human condition.[13] Taking our cue from this description of the authentic Jew, we could infer that for Sartre authenticity in a general sense would fundamentally involve more than having a true and lucid consciousness of some particular historical situation. It would involve more basically the clear awareness of the true universal condition of man—for example, all men are in fact equal, and none has intrinsic rights over others—and the acceptance of the responsibility to live according to this awareness.

Now, it seems to me that the authentic man described above is the same as the man of good faith who Sartre says in *Existentialism and Humanism* chooses freedom as his ultimate goal. (Sartre uses "good faith" and "authenticity" interchangeably in that work.)[14] If authenticity fundamentally involves clearly seeing what is the case and accepting the responsibilities involved therein—and it is the case that all values are created by human freedom—then authenticity involves seeing this, rejecting the spirit of seriousness, and accepting the responsibility for this free creation. We saw at the end of *Being and Nothingness* that the rejection of God as man's ultimate value could come about once man saw and accepted the truth concerning the human condition: freedom alone is the source of all values. The individual who sees and accepts the responsibility involved in that state of affairs is precisely the authentic individual. Note, by the way, that it is not authenticity itself in isolation that is the ultimate value here; freedom is. Authenticity is a relative term; an individual must be authentic about something, either a particular state of affairs or the general human condition, or both. To speak as if authenticity itself is the ultimate value in Sartrean ethics is to speak of an abstraction, and a rather empty one at that.[15] "Authentic" is simply the term used here to designate the individual who in clear awareness of his freedom as the source of all value accepts his responsibility for this and chooses freedom as his ultimate value.

However, it is still not clear why an authentic individual's acceptance of his responsibility for his free creation of values entails the choice of freedom over everything else as his ultimate value. Recall one of the major objections we discussed in detail in the last chapter. We pointed out that critics such as Bernstein and Warnock have maintained that since Sartre holds that no values are objective the only ethics (if it can be so designated) possible for him is one of complete individualism and relativism. "If objective values are dead, everything is permitted." On what basis, then, can Sartre single out freedom as his ultimate value? Neither it, nor the acceptance of responsibility, nor authenticity has any objective value. Of course, if someone does choose any of these, they thereby become valuable for him. But why choose them? Why not choose pleasure, fame, power, virtue, even bad faith, as the ultimate value? It would seem that a selection of any number of attainable goals in place of being God would render man's life meaningful. If nothing has any objective or intrinsic value, there would appear to be no reason, other than an individual's own whim, to prefer freedom over other possibilities. Yet Sartre specifically proposes that choice as the alternative to choosing to value being God. To see how he can legitimately do so, we must look closely at those passages in which he argues for the primacy of this goal. Though he does not thoroughly present his reasoning, its general direction is clear; and by supplementing his words with those of de Beauvoir, we can arrive at a rather complete presentation.

In *Existentialism and Humanism* Sartre attempts to reply to various charges made against his existentialism, among them the charge that his position disallows the possibility of making any judgments about the moral good or evil of anyone's conduct. If there are no objective moral values such judgments are meaningless, the objection contends. Sartre's reply is as follows:

> . . . the attitude of strict consistency alone is that of good faith. Furthermore, I can pronounce a moral judgment. For I declare that freedom, in respect of concrete circumstances, can have no other end and aim but itself; and when once a man has seen that values depend upon himself, in that state of forsakenness he can will only one thing, and that is freedom as the foundation of all values. . . . the actions of men of good faith have, as their ultimate significance, the quest of freedom itself as such.[16]

Good faith (authenticity) is the attitude of strict consistency, and is the choice of freedom itself. Apparently, Sartre considers the choice of freedom to be most consistent with the human condition and the nature of value, since human freedom alone is the source of all value. Incidentally, the similarity between this brief argument and Sartre's even briefer statements at the end of *Being and Nothingness* should not be ignored. In the latter, after rejecting the spirit of seriousness, he asks, "is it possible for freedom to take itself for a value as the source of all value . . . ?"[17] The suggestion, though brief, seems again to be that since freedom is the source of all values it should be chosen as the ultimate value.

Let us attempt to develop a little more fully what Sartre

is proposing so cryptically here, paying particular attention to his emphasis on consistency. Suppose someone were to choose pleasure or fame or even bad faith as the ultimate value of his life. Any of these would, of course, become a value for him, but only because he had freely made it such. Now, once a person realizes, Sartre suggests, that it is only due to freedom that any of these is a value, it is most *consistent* with this state of affairs for him to choose freedom (rather than pleasure, fame, or bad faith) as his ultimate value. His reference to consistency can also be understood in a logical sense. Thus he may be arguing that, since freedom is ontologically entailed in all values as their source, the choice of any and all values logically entails the prior valuing of freedom. These suggestions have a certain force, but the argument is so briefly set forth by Sartre that it will be helpful to turn to de Beauvoir's *Ethics* for her expression of it.

At the basis of her presentation of the argument is her agreement with Sartre that all men desire to give meaning and value to their existence to justify it. As we have seen, the fact that all men desire to be God means they naturally seek this justification. But this justification, she claims, can come about only if man makes freedom his supreme value. Thus, she says, "Freedom is the source from which all significations and all values spring. It is the original condition of all justification of existence. The man who seeks to justify his life must want freedom itself absolutely and above everything else."[18] The argument is clearly parallel to Sartre's. Like him, de Beauvoir considers freedom as the source of all meaning and value, all justification, of existence. It follows from this that I must value freedom itself if any valuation it gives to my life is to be ultimately meaningful. De Beauvoir points out that if freedom were to deny value to itself "it would deny the possibility of any foundation," in the sense of justification, for my existence. Her reasoning is that in the choice of anything as a value there is logically entailed the more fundamental choice of freedom as a value; otherwise that choice of anything else as a value would itself be radically repudiated. To put it succinctly, if I do not value my freedom how could I consistently value any value it creates, including the valuation or justification it gives to my own existence? Note clearly that neither existentialist is claiming that freedom should be chosen because it possesses some intrinsic objective value. Quite the contrary, the argument is that it is precisely because nothing, including freedom, has objective value, because all values come only from freedom, that freedom should be chosen above all. Note, then, how Sartre's ontology, specifically his subjectivistic view of value, provides the very basis for this argument, rather than rendering his ethics impossible, as critics claim. Only by valuing freedom first and foremost will any of the values it subsequently creates be meaningful or justified, including the value it places on my own existence. Thus de Beauvoir asserts, "To will oneself moral [in context this means to will to justify one's life] and to will oneself free are one and the same decision."[19]

Of course, even by valuing freedom man will not attain the necessary meaning and self-justification of a God. Furthermore, his choice to value freedom will not cause some intrinsic meaning or value to accrue to his human existence. In the Sartrean universe, as we have said, it is up to man alone, more precisely to his freedom, to create a meaningful and so justified existence for himself. For man, de Beauvoir says, "it is not a matter of being right in the eyes of a God [or of any objective values], but of being right in his own eyes."[20] To be sure, any value man chooses to center his life around will give his life some meaning and justification. But man can best be "right," he can best justify his life, by choosing freedom as his ultimate value. Such a choice is best because it is most consistent with the way things are and most consistent logically. So argue Sartre and de Beauvoir.

B. Objections

Though some commentators appear to be unaware that Sartre and de Beauvoir actually advance arguments to support their proposal that freedom should be man's primary value,[21] a number of others have confronted their reasoning and judged it to be wanting. Bernstein, for example, considers the argument "feeble," apparently because it hinges on a prior decision to value logical consistency.[22] Recall that Sartre maintains that the choice of freedom is the most consistent choice in light of the fact that freedom is the source of all values, and de Beauvoir says in effect the same thing. The point is, and Bernstein is correct in noting it, consistency in itself has no intrinsic or objective value in Sartre's ontology. Man is under no obligation, moral or otherwise, to be consistent. But if this is so, then he can be under no obligation to choose freedom as his primary value. Bernstein further criticizes Sartre for unjustifiably deriving moral value from a factual state of affairs that in itself lacks any value.[23] That is, simply because freedom is in fact the source of all values, it does not follow that man must or should take it as a value. Another critic, Henry Veatch, puts this objection clearly:

> Supposing that man is free, why should the mere fact that he is so make it wrong for him to pretend that he is not, or to try to conceal from himself his true condition? Is this not to derive an "ought" or an "ought not" from an "is"? . . . from the fact that the existentialist fancies that he has discovered that man has the property of being free [how] can he infer that man is under obligation to make choices in full recognition and acknowledgment of that freedom?[24]

Sartre himself would apparently have to agree with this, for, as we saw in chapter 2, he certainly insists upon the impossibility of identifying values and facts. Merely because something is the case in no way requires that it be taken as an ideal (value) to be sought. Recall that Sartre maintains that the fact that man desires to be God does not mean that he must choose this desire or its fulfillment as values. Similarly, the fact that man is ontologically the free source of all his values does not require him to confer value on his freedom. As he himself says, "ontology itself cannot formulate ethical precepts."[25]

Other criticisms of Sartre's and de Beauvoir's position do not focus on their argument but on the intelligibility of their assertion that freedom should be man's supreme value. Though both existentialists insist that this choice is not of some abstraction but of freedom concretely situated,[26] they have often been reproached with proposing a vague, almost contentless ideal. Furthermore, as we saw, since Sartre holds that value is that which is to be made real, and since in his ontology man is said to be already free by nature as well as in his choices, what sense is there in advising him to value freedom? Critics as different as Gabriel Marcel and contemporary Marxists have raised this objection.[27] Does not Sartre himself claim that "the slave in chains is as free as his master"[28] and "there is no situation in which the for-itself would be *more free* than in others"?[29] If man is in reality free in all situations why advise him to value freedom, since to value it means to choose to make it real? Along the same line, there are critics who have maintained that, because freedom is omnipresent for Sartre, every choice of every value will turn out to be morally good—precisely because every choice is free—even, say, the choice to value a life of bad faith.[30] This, of course, would make any distinction between morally good and morally bad choices meaningless.

Let me sum up these diverse criticisms in the following five objections. The first two deal directly with the argument offered by Sartre and de Beauvoir, which is given above in section A.

1. It is claimed that the argument fails because it rests on the presupposition that consistency must be taken as a value, and this, of course, is false in the light of Sartre's insistence that things are of value only if I choose them to be.

2. The argument invalidly attempts to derive values from facts. This is inconsistent with Sartre's view that the two are radically distinct and that ontology cannot supply moral precepts.

The other objections focus on the intelligibility of proposing freedom as a value.

3. Since values for Sartre are ideals to be made real, and

since man is by nature already free, it makes no sense to encourage him to value freedom.

4. Because all of man's choices are free, if freedom is man's primary moral value this will mean that all of his choices will inevitably have moral worth.

5. Finally, a general criticism, probably not totally different from the two preceding, is that the freedom that these existentialists propose as a value is simply too formal and lacking in content to supply any moral direction.

A consideration of these objections in the following section makes it clearer what Sartre and de Beauvoir mean by the choice to value freedom, and exactly what force they see in the argument they advance to support this choice.

C. SARTRE'S AND DE BEAUVOIR'S RESPONSES

The first two objections given above can be dealt with together. It should be noted from the beginning that the argument for freedom, given in section A, is based, not so much on the fact that man is free as on the belief that men desire to attain a meaningful or justified existence. De Beauvoir's version of the argument shows this clearly, for she proposes the choice of freedom precisely because she believes that through it man can best justify his life and attain meaning for it. Of course, the argument further presupposes that man values his desire for a meaningful existence and such an existence itself. For, if he had that desire but did not value its goal, then the reasons offered for the choice of freedom would be of no significance to him. Once a person chooses to justify his life, de Beauvoir and Sartre can plausibly argue, the best way to do so is by choosing freedom above all else. The question is, can any reason be given as to why he should value a meaningful or justified life in the first place? Would any reason offered inevitably involve an illicit attempt to move from facts to values, as the critics charge?

There is no doubt that both existentialists consider it obvious that men do desire to attain a meaningful existence.

No external obligation forces man to seek meaning; "he finds within himself the anxious question, 'What's the use?' " de Beauvoir writes.[31] She adds, "He flees it only by fleeing himself, and as soon as he exists he answers." In other words, man in fact does desire meaning, he is continually choosing his life's projects and values, values which give his existence some justification. In a sense, then, the question is not whether men should or should not value a meaningful existence—they do value it. Just as men are "condemned" to be free, so they are condemned to seek meaning and justification. While this is true, the value of a meaningful existence, inasmuch as it is desired, is only the kind of value Sartre calls a nonreflective or lived value. And on this level man also values being God. Yet, as I said in the previous chapter, the mere fact something is a nonreflective value does not mean it must be reflectively freely chosen as a value. Just as men can and should freely refuse upon reflection to value the impossible goal of being God, Sartre believes, so also they could upon reflection freely refuse to value a meaningful existence. Our question is, then, more precisely, can any reason be given why men should reflectively freely value a meaningful or justified life? It is true that, while the goal to be God is unattainable, the goal to create a meaningful existence is attainable. Nevertheless, this is not a compelling reason for freely valuing it. Indeed, can any reason be given for doing so without involving one in the so-called naturalistic fallacy?

In the final analysis I believe both Sartre and de Beauvoir would grant that no logically compelling reason that would prove that a man ought to value a meaningful existence can be supplied. As we have seen, Sartre is well aware that the data of ontology, in this case man's desire for meaning, cannot of itself supply the value for ethics.[32] In spite of what Sartre's critics say he is not guilty of deriving, or attempting to derive, values from facts. The *fact* that man desires meaning for his existence does not logically entail that he must *value* this desired meaning. Furthermore, both Sartre and de Beauvoir explicitly admit that logic and reason themselves have value only if man chooses them to.[33] Thus it is impossible to advance reasons demonstrating that man should value reasons or logical consistency. Obviously, unless I value rationality in the first place, no reasons or logical argumentation can persuade me to do so. It is also obvious that unless I value logic and rationality no argument using them to propose freedom as my primary value will be convincing. However, to admit that no compelling reasons can be offered for valuing logic and rationality or for valuing a meaningful existence is not to say that no reasons at all can be advanced. Man's deep longing for justification and the fact that a meaningful life is attainable are certainly reasons that support the valuing of such a life. Likewise, the fact that no matter what he does man is going to create some meaning for his existence prompts him to value a meaningful life and to create the best possible meaning he can. It can also prompt him to seek a meaning in his life that is internally rational and consistent with the facts of reality, especially the fact that freedom is the source of all value. Still, it remains the case that an individual (like Dostoevsky's underground man, perhaps) may freely choose not to value the justification of his existence and not to value rationality and consistency with reality. It may be true, as de Beauvoir claims, that such a person is "fleeing himself" and will inevitably create a meaning for his existence. Nevertheless, he may freely value that "flight from self" and choose not to value whatever meaning he gives his life. But this is self-contradictory, one retorts. For the individual in question must value his very refusal to value a meaningful existence, and thereby he gives meaning to his existence. He is in effect valuing a life of refusal and declaring it to be meaningful at the same time that he says he places no value on a meaningful life—a patent contradiction. This may be true, but no matter, for this individual can value this very contradiction—just as a person who strives to be God values a self-contradiction.

Thus, there is no escape from the fact that the choice to value a meaningful and justified life is a free one made without logically compelling reasons: "nothing forces him [man] to try to justify his being." It is also true that no reasons force him to value consistency and rationality. Still, de Beauvoir goes on, life "is permitted to wish to give itself a meaning and a truth, and it then meets rigorous demands within its own heart,"[34] the demands, I take it, that rationality and consistency with reality be valued and that freedom be chosen above all else. Though this goes a long way toward answering critics of their argument, difficulties remain in this response. I will discuss these in the next section.

As for the objections that question the intelligibility of proposing freedom as a value, one of them (number 4) can be handled rather quickly. Sartre would claim that it rests on a fundamental misunderstanding of how freedom functions as the supreme value in his ethics. Though his ontology maintains that all men's choices are free and that all create value, even the choice to live in bad faith, this does not mean that all are morally equivalent. Sartrean ethics is not simply asking men to choose freely and to create value freely, as these critics seem to assume. After all, men do that already. His ethics advocates the choice of freedom as man's ultimate value. Men often hide from their freedom and choose to consider themselves determined by circumstances and/or bound by objective values. Men often choose being God as their highest value. The authentic person is not only one who chooses freely; he is not only one who freely creates values— all men always do both. He is one who freely chooses to value freedom above all else—and few men do that, Sartre believes.

Still, if man is already free by nature in his basic structure, what sense is there in advocating that he choose freedom as his basic value (objection number 3)? In giving these existentialists' replies we should point out that they distinguish between freedom as referring to the very structure of man, and human freedom as referring to man's choices and acts.[35] Freedom in the first sense, as we saw in the previous chapter, refers to man's ontological structure as radically different from things—a structure that is the very condition of his detachment from being, of his ability to transcend what-is and grasp what-is-not. As radically different from things, man (or more precisely, the for-itself) can never be totally bound and determined by the causal order of things. It is true that all men possess this basic structure and so are able to transcend what-is in their choices. In this sense the slave in chains can be said to be as free as his master. Still, Sartre and de Beauvoir point out, man is able to choose what value to give this structural freedom. Men often choose to reject it or hide from it in pretending they are by nature determined. What the critics themselves seem to forget is that simply because something, in this case freedom, is a fact does not make it valuable. These existentialists call for man to value the freedom that is his very structure.[36] They ask him to acknowledge his freedom, to accept the fact that he is the source of values and cannot abrogate this responsibility, and to strive to live accordingly. But what does it mean—"to live accordingly"? Here we come to the second sense of freedom, freedom as referring to choices and acts.

Recall the argument of section A, which claimed that man should take freedom as his ultimate value because freedom is in fact the source of all meaning and value. Now, what freedom is in fact this source? Most proximately, it is man's freedom of choice, for by his choices he creates all his values, except for his nonreflective value, God. It follows, then, according to the argument, that he should value not only his structure as a free being, but also his freedom of choice. This means that man should choose to remove restrictions to this freedom—for example, ignorance—and to increase positively the range of choices available to him. Though both may be ontologically free, the slave in chains obviously does not have the same range of options to choose from as does his master. Though freedom of choice is always present to him, since he can say yes or no to the options he does have, the slave's freedom of choice is clearly quite limited in scope. To increase this freedom would mean, for one thing, to increase his awareness of the options from which he could choose. Even more importantly, it would mean to make more options actually available to him. To achieve this would in turn require changing the structure of the world in which he lives so as to offer him more real possibilities for choice.[37] A man immersed in poverty, disease, and ignorance obviously has fewer choices and fewer possibilities that he can realistically hope to attain than a man blessed with wealth, health, and knowledge. If I value the former's freedom of choice, then I must work to improve his situation so that his poverty, disease, and ignorance are overcome and more goals are within his grasp. I emphasize this point lest someone get the impression that to value freedom of choice means simply to value a purely mental act. Traditionally, a distinction has been drawn between freedom of choice and freedom of action, the latter referring to freedom to attain goals sought. While this distinction is valid, for one can freely choose to do something and yet be unable to do it, it should not be made into a separation. To speak of freedom of choice as independent of freedom of action is to make an erroneous abstraction. Some critics seem to do just this, for they write as if the freedom that Sartre takes as his supreme value is a freedom of choice in almost total isolation from freedom to attain goals sought.[38] Freedom of choice is in reality inseparable from freedom to attain goals; thus, to value the former demands valuing the latter and consequently valuing the modification of the situation so as to broaden the attainable goals. I should add parenthetically that Sartre himself was guilty in *Being and Nothingness* of overly separating man's freedom of choice from freedom to attain goals —"success is not important to freedom," he wrote there.[39] He has since admitted that his realization of the situated and engaged side to human freedom was very incomplete in 1943. Only gradually did he become aware of the tremendous power of the situation to limit or enhance freedom.[40]

In any case it is clear that Sartre never thought there was any incompatibility between insisting that man was ontologically free and at the same time advocating that he choose to realize his freedom more fully and concretely. In reply to Marxist critics he states, "if man is not originally [i.e., ontologically] free, but determined once and for all, we cannot even conceive what his liberation might be."[41] In other words, if man is by nature determined, if he is chained to things and is merely the result of their causal forces, then to speak of his becoming free (as the Marxists do) or increasing his freedom concretely is almost nonsensical. True, his situation could be improved so that he can more readily attain the goals of his choices and desires. His freedom to attain could be increased. Still, if his nature is such that his very choices and desires remain the determined product of causal forces, he remains ontologically no more than a robot.

I have argued that to choose freedom as the ultimate value means to work to remove restrictions to choice and to the attainment of goals sought, according to Sartre and de Beauvoir. Clearly, then, any repressive political, social, economic, religious, etc., policies or systems would be intolerable. On the positive side all acts, policies, or systems that serve to enhance freedom of choice by promoting dissemination of knowledge and by enabling man to attain his goals would be supported. This is still quite general, of course, and must be made more specific if these existentialists are to reply adequately to the fifth objection, which claimed that freedom as a goal was simply too vague to furnish any moral direction. Actually, there is some force to this complaint because Sartre and de Beauvoir have in fact tended to be much clearer on what they believe man should be free *from* than on what he should be free *for*—to introduce a traditional distinction.

Anyone familiar with the many political and social essays and books of these two knows that in general they have striven to free man from all political oppression, whether socialist or capitalist in form, from deceit and enforced ignorance, from exploitation of man by man, such as colonialism, sexism, racism, classism—the list could go on and on. De Beauvoir's autobiographies, as well as the works by Jeanson and the bibliographical life by Contat and Rybalka, contain ample details of their activities in behalf of human liberation. Whether one agrees with their political and social views or not, he must acknowledge that few philosophers of our time have been as publicly committed to the causes they believe in. Clearly, the freedom they advocate, freedom from oppression in all its forms, is not vague or contentless, as the critics claim. It is specified and gains content *vis-à-vis* the very forces it strives to be liberated from. As Sartre says, "what counts in this case is the particular form of the obstacle to surmount, of the resistance to overcome. That is what gives form to freedom in each circumstance."[42] But what about freedom in a positive sense? What is liberated freedom for; what is its goal? To say that it is for freedom is not very enlightening.

To give content to the choice of freedom as a positive goal, Sartre's and de Beauvoir's insistence that the choice is of freedom concretely situated should be recalled. Most commentators have interpreted this to mean that freedom must be seen as determinately located in the world. This is true, of course, but the most immediate situation in which freedom is found concretely is in human beings themselves, human beings with their specific facticity. After all, it is *human* freedom that we are concerned with. Now, an absolutely fundamental dimension of human facticity that must be understood if we are to comprehend man and the goals he pursues is the dimension of *needs*, Sartre says in his *Critique of Dialectical Reason*. Men seek what they do because of their needs: "need . . . is in fact the lived revelation of a goal to aim at."[43] While needs may vary somewhat from one individual to another, there are basic ones common to all men, to all who share in what Sartre calls the universal human "condition."[44] Though he is famous for denying that man has a built-in "essence," Sartre has always insisted that there is a "truth" about man as such, not just about individuals; that there is a universal structure common to all; that "certain original structures are invariable and in each For-itself which constitute human reality."[45] (Actually, by "essence" he seems to mean a very *specific* set of features, preprogrammed tendencies, desires, etc., which are present in animals. It is this essence, and not common *general* features, that he denies is in man.)[46] It is man's needs, especially his common human needs, that give content to the ethical choice of human freedom concretely situated.

It was argued above that to value man's freedom of choice is to seek to provide him with more real possibilities from which he can choose, and that this in turn requires that he be enabled to attain more goals. Now, since man's goals, according to Sartre, are determined and specified by his needs, then to value man's freedom of choice means to value the fulfillment of his needs, especially those which are part of the structure common to all men. Thus, to promote man's freedom in a positive sense would be primarily to assist him in being free for the attainment of those goals that he naturally seeks in order to fulfill his needs.[47] It would be to aid him in fulfilling his basic needs, such as those for food, shelter, warmth, sex, etc., and in continually striving to fulfill his more specifically human needs through pursuits such as science, art, technology, philosophy, etc. Put simply, it would be to seek continually to develop human existence in all its multifaceted features. (I say "continually develop" because, as de Beauvoir points out, part of the human condition seems to be that there is no fixed limit to the amount of knowledge, beauty, companionship, etc., man can attain.)[48] De Beauvoir speaks of a time when oppression will be eliminated and "men will know no other use of their freedom than this free unfurling of itself." This is a time, she says, in which science, art, technology, and all of man's endeavors will have as their goal "the opening of ever new possibilities for man," the goal in other words of "pursuing the expansion of his existence and of retrieving this very effort as an absolute."[49] In the same vein Sartre refers to man's ideal as "play," a state that "has freedom for its foundation and its goal." Man plays for the sheer joy of playing; he seeks no external goal but simply to exercise and develop his free existence.[50] The choice of human freedom, of course, would not ignore individual differences in the way men possess their basic human needs, nor the different ways they "play"—that is, pursue the expansion of their existence. Nevertheless, the choice gains content in Sartre's and de Beauvoir's thought not simply from the individuality of a person's needs and goals but more basically from the fact that he is an individual *human* being, and therefore possesses generally specifiable *human* needs and goals.

D. CRITICAL EVALUATION

I begin this section by commenting on the preceding discussion, which covered Sartre's and de Beauvoir's replies to the objection that their proposed value, freedom, is vague and contentless. There is some truth to this charge, though their ideal is not nearly as vague as some critics believe. Certainly, they do not just set forth the obscure proposal that the goal in ethics is freedom for the sake of freedom. The preceding analysis, especially insofar as it contained Sartre's concept of needs and linked the choice of freedom to the choice to fulfill human needs, seems to me to be very fruitful. To make human freedom man's primary value is to propose as a goal the progressive and never-ending attaining of those ends that man naturally seeks because of his needs. In fact, this goal, far from being as vacuous as critics claim, is common to the entire Western humanistic tradition. It is the unlimited expansion and development of the human being in all his capacities; and Sartre does call his ideal "true and positive humanism."[51] Still, something is lacking in his analysis.

Missing in his treatment of needs is any suggestion as to how one determines what man's needs are and, especially, what his real needs are as opposed to false or artificial ones. Sartre himself distinguishes genuine from "artificially created" needs, and advocates the fulfilling of the former in preference to the latter.[52] He criticizes those who consider, for example, their need for a car greater than their need for health. And he clearly does not believe that man should attempt to fulfill all the needs he thinks he has. Some people feel a need to use others sadistically, some feel a need to self-destruct. No doubt these are false needs in Sartre's eyes, and it would be better overall not to fulfill them. Yet the fact remains that he offers no detail on how to distinguish such needs from real needs.

Furthermore, since both kinds of needs are part of a given human being's facticity, it is not clear why Sartre gives preference to the fulfillment of real needs rather than of false ones. Recall the above argument connecting freedom and the fulfillment of needs. It pointed out that to value man's freedom of choice entails seeking to provide him with more attainable goals from which to choose. Since his goals are in turn determined by his needs, to value freedom of choice entails valuing the attainment of goals that fulfill needs. But since all of man's needs, whether real or artificial, specify the goals he seeks, it seems arbitrary for Sartre to place primacy on attaining goals that fulfill genuine human needs. After all, if man freely chooses to value only the fulfillment of his artificial needs (presuming that that is possible), it would be only these and not his real needs that would have value. It is not that I disagree with Sartre's preference; I think he is correct. I simply wish to point out that he offers no argument to justify it.

In speaking of content in Sartrean ethics, we should also note that, according to the foregoing, the moral value of man's actions and the moral obligation to do an act are, of course, determined by the consequences this action has for freedom. In general, morally good or right acts are those that increase concrete freedom, either negatively by lessening restrictions of it or positively by increasing man's ability to choose and thus his power to attain the goals he seeks.[53] Recall in this connection that I noted at the beginning of this chapter that Sartre seems to believe that all values are moral in character. This should be clearer now, for if it is true it means that all values bear some relation to freedom, either enhancing or diminishing it. And exactly the same thing could be said of man's acts. Note that I am speaking here of the morality of actions, not of the moral character of the person who acts. Certainly, everyone who performs a morally good act increasing freedom is not thereby a morally good person, nor thereby "authentic"—to use Sartre's term. Even a person in bad faith, as well as one simply in ignorance, could perform a morally good act. The authentic individual, as we saw earlier, is one who (1) acts for freedom, (2) has at the same time "a true and lucid consciousness of the situation" in which he is, and (3) accepts responsibility for his act. The man of bad faith lacks one or more of these characteristics. In any case, since it determines the morality of an action itself by its consequences for freedom, Sartrean ethics is clearly teleological in nature, like so many traditional ethical theories. I suspect that those who label it deontological are either considering authenticity in abstraction from freedom or taking the value of freedom itself in too abstract a sense, perhaps because they radically separate freedom of choice from freedom to attain goals sought.[54] (They may do this because they concentrate too exclusively on Sartre's early works in which he himself is occasionally guilty of this.) Thus they fail to take seriously enough the ethical ramifications of both Sartre's and de Beauvoir's insistence that the choice of freedom is a choice of freedom concretely situated in human facticity in the world. Needless to say, they have also failed to consider seriously the ethical implications of these existentialists' many activities of a social and political nature, which illustrate in practice their choice of freedom.

I would like to turn once again to a consideration of Sartre's notion of value. In the preceding chapter, I argued that he arbitrarily adopted an overly narrow concept inasmuch as he defined values as nonreal ideals to be made real. I suggested that we should be alert to see if he is able to maintain this restricted meaning. An analysis of some of his arguments set forth in the preceding section shows clearly that it is not maintained. There seems to be significant ambiguity in the way both he and de Beauvoir explain what it means to choose to value freedom. This ambiguity arises because they are not consistent in the way they use the term "value." Thus, for example, when they speak of choosing to value man's freedom of choice, this means apparently to choose to value the *increase* of this freedom, to choose to make

61

it more real. Likewise, choosing to value the fulfillment of human needs means to choose to value the continual increase of their fulfillment. This is consistent with Sartre's notion of value, set forth in chapter 2, in which values are described as ideals that call for their realization. Given that meaning, to choose to value something would mean to bring it from the ideal level to that of being, to try to make it real or more real. But when Sartre and de Beauvoir argue against their critics (objection number 3 above) that it makes sense to exhort man to value his ontological freedom—his very structure as a free being—they cannot be using the notions of value and choosing to value in the same way. To choose to value this structure cannot mean to attempt to increase it or make it more real, for it is as real as it can be. This is the freedom Sartre says is whole and entire in every man. To value it means, rather, to accept willingly the fact that one is fundamentally free, not to hide from it. Clearly, in this case the notion of value is not restricted to a nonreal ideal to be made real, since it is applied to something already real. Of course, as I said earlier, this use of the term is perfectly correct. Surely I can value a present, or for that matter a past, pleasurable experience or situation without seeking, or even being able, to increase it so as to make it more real. The problem is that Sartre's definition of value does not allow this. In any case Sartre and de Beauvoir are simply not consistent; they move without justification from one notion of value to another and from one meaning of "choosing to value" to another. This has serious effects on the basic argument they offer to demonstrate that man should value freedom since it is the source of all values. At the most, their argument shows that man should value free choice as well as the structure in which it is rooted, but that is all it shows. It does not show that man should value or strive to *increase* this free choice, unless, again, one makes the assumption that values are always ideals to be made real or more real—thus, to value something necessarily entails choosing to make it more real. To summarize my criticism: at best these existentialists have demonstrated that man should choose to value his condition as a being free by nature and able to choose freely within concrete situations. They have not established that man must strive to increase or make more real this free choice by modifying the situation so as to increase options available to him.

I referred just now to the argument these existentialists offer to show that freedom should be chosen as man's supreme value, and I now address myself to it and to its critics. In the first place, I think that it is wrong to charge Sartre and de Beauvoir with moving illegitimately from facts to values (objection number 2 above). Actually, Sartre's reasoning in *Existentialism and Humanism* is so briefly given that it is impossible to be sure just what moves he makes. But de Beauvoir's expanded version makes it clear that they are not guilty of the naturalistic fallacy. Both are fully aware that the fact that man is free, as well as the more basic fact that he seeks a meaningful existence, does not logically require him to value either that existence or his freedom. They are also equally aware that logic and consistency with reality have no intrinsic value (objection number 1 above). They admit that there are no compelling reasons to value a meaningful existence, logical consistency, or consistency with reality. Granting all this, the fact is that the argument they offer does work, provided one initially chooses to value a meaningful life and consistency. If man wants the latter, and Sartre and de Beauvoir believe he naturally does, and if it is the case that freedom and nothing else is the source of all values, then it is most consistent with this state of affairs to choose freedom itself as one's primary value. As de Beauvoir points out, the choice to value freedom is logically entailed in the choice to value anything else. If one does not value freedom first and foremost, no value that it gives to anything, including the value it gives to one's own life, ultimately has any significance for him. I have no difficulty with the internal movement of this reasoning, once the prerequisite value choices are made. (However, as I just said, to value freedom does not necessarily entail valuing its increase.) The hitch lies elsewhere.

As I read their argument, or more precisely de Beauvoir's much more thorough version, it appears to assume that once man values the attainment of a meaningful existence he must at the same time value logic and consistency with reality. But I see no necessary connection. Even if man does value attaining a meaningful existence, this does not require him to value the latter. A meaningful existence, one that has value, can be achieved by valuing irrationality (recall Dostoevsky's underground man) or nonrationality (e.g., a life based on following the emotional whim of the moment—if it feels good, do it!), or even by valuing escape from reality (e.g., drugs). If a person chooses to value one of the above lives it has value, it has meaning. Granted, it is in fact the individual's freedom that creates such values. Freedom is at the root of them all. Granted too, that it would be more consistent for him to value this freedom; it would be illogical for him to value the goals freedom chooses and yet not to value freedom itself. But such appeals to consistency and logic have force only on one who has chosen to value consistency with facts and logical entailments. And there seem to be no compelling reasons why one must so choose. Since, as we saw, Sartre and de Beauvoir clearly do not presume logic and consistency to be of intrinsic value, they must believe that in the choice of a meaningful life, a life having value, there is included the choice of logic and consistency with reality. Unfortunately, they do not attempt to show this, and I am at a loss to do so.

The only explicit discussion of this point that I have found in the Sartrean literature is that offered by Hazel Barnes, one of Sartre's most knowledgeable and sympathetic commentators. She maintains that the choice to justify man's existence does involve the choice of logical consistency as well as fidelity to reality, for, she asserts, to fail to be logical and/or faithful is to reject what is of "greater positive value."[55] The difficulty with this is that it sounds perilously close to saying that some values are objectively better than others. If man creates all values then it is he alone who decides which "positive" values are greater, and he can decide that inconsistency and infidelity are. This fact—that there seems to be no necessary connection between a meaningful life and consistency—causes serious problems for this ethics in other areas, as we shall see.

If we were to leave Sartrean ethics at this point, we could easily give the impression that it is a morality of the most *laissez-faire* type. Each man is to choose his freedom, the continual expansion of his own existence, and that's the end to it. Some have interpreted Sartre to be advocating exactly this, and so they have claimed that his ethics is a license for radical individualism, and that its logical result is chaos and anarchy. There is some basis for this if one sticks simply to *Being and Nothingness,* for the choice of freedom as value briefly suggested there does seem to be a highly individual matter. Still, such interpretations run counter to the fact that the writings and efforts of Sartre and de Beauvoir since 1943 do not show that they believe that just any act done for the sake of a person's own freedom is justified, nor that each man in his search for freedom can disregard others. Such interpretations also ignore the fact that both existentialists have come to reject the idea that morality is primarily an individual matter; they insist that "no individual salvation is possible."[56] What needs to be explained, then, is the social dimension of the value of freedom in Sartrean ethics. What should be the relation of one man's freedom to another's, according to this moral theory? If I am to take freedom as my supreme value, and so is everyone else, what moral obligations to others does this entail in a social milieu of inevitably interacting freedoms?

4

The Social Dimension
of the Value of Freedom

A. THE OBJECTIONS

We have already mentioned that Sartre himself has admitted
that he has progressed from a very individualistic conception
of freedom and salvation to an awareness of the social dimension of both. In *Being and Nothingness* he seemed to consider the choice of freedom to be primarily an individual
matter, even going so far as to say that no man could increase
or decrease the freedom of another.[1] In that work Sartre
appeared most interested in explaining why free human beings do not choose their freedom but flee from it in pursuing
a type of existence incompatible with it—namely, by adopting the spirit of seriousness and living in bad faith.[2] The
alternative he proposed at that time was for an individual to
undergo a "radical conversion" and choose to face up to and
accept his freedom as his goal by renouncing his vain attempts
to be God. The fact that the situation of many men was such
as to render this choice almost impossible was practically
ignored. And what the relation should be between authentic
individuals, each choosing his own freedom, was never discussed.

It is true that in later works such as *Saint Genet* and

Critique of Dialectical Reason Sartre very thoroughly explored the situated character of human freedom, especially its presence in the social world of many freedoms. He stressed the alienated state of human freedom in our world, the limitations to which it is subject, and the corresponding need for cooperation among men if they are truly to advance the realm of freedom. Personal salvation is impossible, he now insists, for no individual can solely by his own efforts achieve a fully free existence.[3] However, in spite of this emphasis on the social dimension of freedom the fact remains, and critics have noted it, that neither in the *Critique* nor in any other work has Sartre taken pains to advance arguments to demonstrate clearly man's moral obligation to any freedom other than his own. In the 1950s he discussed with de Beauvoir the tension he felt between the requirements of freedom on the one hand and the need for community on the other; between his desire to safeguard his personal liberty and his need for others.[4] It may be that he has never fully resolved this tension, at least in his philosophical writings, which explains the inadequacy just mentioned.

Most commentators recognize that in *Existentialism and Humanism* Sartre does propose what he considers to be man's moral responsibility to others. He says there, "I am obliged to will the freedom of others at the same time as mine. I cannot make freedom my aim unless I make that of others equally my aim."[5] His reasons for holding this remain unclear. Why am I obliged to will not just my own personal freedom but equally that of others? The brief suggestions Sartre makes in support of his position are woefully inadequate, critics claim.

Since in section B we analyze Sartre's arguments, brief as they are, in detail, I forgo at this time any further elaboration of this complaint. Once we have set forth his reasoning we will be in a better position to see the force of the objection.

There is yet another serious charge often raised against Sartre's contention that men are obliged to will the freedom of others. This is the objection that his ontology, specifically his view of the nature of human relations set forth in *Being and Nothingness,* renders unintelligible any exhortation or command to choose the freedom of others.

In his early work Sartre maintains, according to numerous critics, that all human relations are relations of conflict.[6] In great detail he describes many relations and shows that in every case, including that of love, they involve conflict inasmuch as they are all attempts at domination and subjection of oneself by others and/or of others by oneself. In fact, at the very beginning of his discussion of the most fundamental concrete human relations he writes, "The following descriptions of concrete behavior must therefore be envisaged within the perspective of *conflict.* Conflict is the original meaning of being-for-others."[7] And, at the end of this same section, even after investigating the relations among men cooperating and working together, he insists that the result of this investigation "is not of a nature to modify the results of our prior investigations"—namely, that "the essence of the relations between consciousnesses is not the *Mitsein* [being-with others (Heidegger)]; it is conflict."[8] (In this connection one could recall perhaps the most famous line ever written by Sartre, "Hell is other people.") This means, according to many critics, that it is in principle impossible for conflict ever to be overcome, for it is rooted in Sartre's ontology. A recent commentator, George Stack, puts this well:

> Even assuming that the most ideal economic conditions existed or that complete social justice were attained in a utopian world, there could be no way in which the opposition and hostility Sartre ascribes to the relation between the individual and the other could be overcome since it is an essential ontological trait of the being of man.[9]

If this is so, if Sartre's ontology concludes that all social relations are fundamentally and essentially relations of conflict, how can his exhortation to make the freedom of others one's goal make any sense? It is not enough to dismiss this criticism by saying that Sartre has always tended to accentuate the negative in human affairs. Though this is true it does not address itself to the real issue—the claim that his ontology makes conflict so pervasive in human relations that moral obligations to others become irrelevant. Mary Warnock is one who thinks this is the case. She writes: "If ethics . . . is concerned with the fitting together of the interests and choices of one person with those of another, there is no way into the subject at all if our aim is *necessarily* to dominate the other person and subordinate his freedom to our own."[10] Of course, if his aim is the same as ours, conflict is inevitable.

To explain this objection more adequately, I now propose to analyze in some detail Sartre's statements about conflict in *Being and Nothingness* to see exactly what he means and why he claims it is fundamental in human relations. This analysis is composed of two parts. First, though every single statement Sartre makes on the subject cannot be considered, I in general analyze those passages in which he initially proposes that conflict is essential to human relations (part 3, chapter 1, of *Being and Nothingness*). Second, I deal with his detailed discussion of concrete human relations (part 3, chapter 3) in which he clearly does portray all these relations as involving conflict in the sense of hostile attempts at destruction and/or subjugation. It is particularly important to determine the context in which this discussion takes place.

I begin, then, by considering Sartre's initial statements about conflict in human relations. It is crucial to understand exactly what he means here by conflict. To my knowledge he first uses this term in reference to human relations in his discussion of the views of Hegel and Heidegger concerning the existence of other subjects. The first mention of conflict —and it sets the stage for all his future references—occurs while he is voicing his disagreement with Hegel that all consciousnesses are ultimately one in some Absolute Consciousness or Spirit. Sartre insists, "No logical or epistemological optimism can cover the scandal of the plurality of consciousnesses. . . . So long as consciousnesses exist, the separation *and conflict* [emphasis added] of consciousnesses will remain. . . ."[11] Similarly, he opposes himself to Heidegger's notion of *mitsein*, for as Sartre interprets it this means that consciousnesses are ontologically united with each other. He insists, on the contrary, that they are in "a relation of opposition," of negation—meaning fundamentally that one is *not* the other. If we suppress this opposition, this negation, this separation, he asks, "are we not going to fall into a monism?"[12]

It is precisely this that is his major concern, an ontological monism that would nullify individually distinct consciousnesses. And it is to reject this that he stresses the negative relation between consciousnesses. I am the particular individual I am only by not being any other individual: "If in general there is an Other, it is necessary *above all* [emphasis added] that I be the one who is not the Other, and it is in this very negation . . . that I make myself be and that the Other arises as the Other."[13] And again, "The Other exists for consciousness only as a *refused self.*"[14]

Now, if this is the context in which he first uses the term "conflict," exactly what does it mean? It seems clear that he is using this word to emphasize his view that the most basic ontological relation between individuals is "separation," "opposition," "negation," and "refusal," and that all communities of consciousness presuppose this. Obviously, a community of individuals requires a plurality of individuals to begin with. It is precisely in this sense that Sartre says conflict is the *original* meaning of one's relationship to others.[15] He also emphasizes that this separation, negation, etc., is unbridgeable inasmuch as no two individuals can ever become ontologically one, no matter how much they share or how close their friendship. One might, of course, object that the term "conflict" is too negative in its connotation to accurately express Sartre's meaning. It is worth noting that he himself has subsequently criticized his terminology in *Being and Nothingness* as occasionally chosen more for its literary effect than for philosophical precision.[16] Even more to the point, one might also insist that calling the ontological separateness of individuals conflict implies that Sartre believes this separateness tends toward conflict in a more

71

obvious sense of the term. This is no doubt true, but certainly unsupported at this stage of his analysis. Nevertheless, the basic meaning the term possesses in the aforementioned context is clear enough, and it does not mean actual hostility. It refers primarily to the basic ontological separateness of individuals.

A second context in which Sartre speaks of the conflict of consciousness involves the awareness of one consciousness by another. He claims that the fundamental and initial way by which one subject is aware of another ontologically distinct subject is by being his object. Now, for a subject to be seen as an object is for it to be seen as thinglike, as definable and describable simply in terms of its specific characteristics —5'10" tall, black haired, sullen, serious, female, etc. It is not to apprehend the subject as a free conscious being continually transcending its facticity—even its freedom would be seen as simply one characteristic among the others. Thus he calls this objectification of a subject an alienation of one consciousness by another, and even speaks of it as enslavement. Since it is mutual, he also calls it conflict, or slight conflict in one place.[17]

To explain his position here more fully, we should note that Sartre believes that the original relation in which a man becomes aware of the presence of another subject cannot be of a subject-to-subject type because any such face-to-face encounter inevitably objectifies the other subject. And the experience of another as an object is not the experience of him as a subject, as we have said. Of course, I may judge that this particular object before me is a man, a conscious subject, not a manikin or a robot, but to make even this judgment requires that I have at some previous time already experienced the other as a subject. If this previous experience cannot be a face-to-face encounter, this must mean that I first become aware of the other as a subject in some other way. This is precisely what Sartre claims when he asserts that the original way I am aware of another as a subject is by experiencing myself as an object. Since I cannot be an object for myself, to experience myself as an object is also to experience the other as a subject distinct from me.[18]

This view that objectification is the most basic way one is aware of other subjects is central. Since Sartre believes that objectification grasps another subject as thinglike, it makes sense for him to speak of it as an alienation of that subject, as well as its degradation and enslavement. Borrowing language from theology, he also refers to it as man's "original fall" and original experience of guilt. And he emphasizes that "whatever may be my further relations with others, these relations will be only variations on the original theme of my guilt."[19] It is in this context that he also says that no matter what I do to or for another, my alienation of him and thus my "violation" of his freedom is inevitable.[20] Once again Sartre's choice of terms is dramatic but his meaning is clear. Since subjects, whether they try to or not, mutually alienate each other's subjectivity by their objectification of it, and since this alienating objectification is the primal relation between subjects, "conflict is the original meaning of being-for-others."[21] It is true that, like his first use of the term, conflict here does not strictly speaking mean actual hostility or deliberate attempts at domination among men, yet it certainly does imply that alienating objectification tends to conflict in that overt sense. And indeed it does, as we shall see directly.

In *Being and Nothingness* (part 3, chapter 3), under the heading "Concrete Relations with Others," Sartre describes a host of human relations from love to hate in very negative terms. Love, for example, is portrayed as a subtle attempt to dominate and capture the free subjectivity of the beloved. It is this portrayal of love and in general this section of *Being and Nothingness* that Sartre's critics have seized upon. It is crucial to understand why his presentation of human relationships here is so negative. In his two-page introduction to the section Sartre explains that the various attitudes he describes involve the stances an individual takes towards others in light of his alienation by them. He also makes clear that he is discussing these basic attitudes within the context of an individual's attempt to be God. He points out that in each of the attitudes to be described the subjects involved are attempting to overcome their status as contingent, free beings and to achieve the state of a necessary being that would be its own foundation, God. Insofar as another ontologically separate from me makes me his object, he confers on me a dimension of my being that I can never control nor even directly know. Since I am not this other, I am at the mercy of the free evaluations that he makes of me, and I am unable to view myself as he does. Thus, by objectifying me he gives my being a contingent (because based on his freedom), thinglike status that I am not and cannot be the foundation of. Now, insofar as I am trying to overcome my contingency and be a self-founding necessary being (God), I will, of course, attempt to overcome this alienating objectification by the other. And all of the attitudes that Sartre goes on to describe are attempts to do this in one of two ways. On the one hand, by trying to dominate and objectify (or even obliterate) the other subject, I can try to escape from the contingent, thinglike status the other confers on me. If I am successful in making him an object, my alienation will cease, for I cannot be an object for an object. The elimination of all subjects who are not me is what hate attempts. On the other hand, inasmuch as I am attempting to be a being that founds its own being, I can seek not to destroy the other's subjectivity but to use or, better, *merge* with it to overcome our ontological separateness. If I am successful, I will no longer have a dimension of my being, my objectness, outside of my control but will be the very foundation of it. For I will be the (other) subject who is conferring it. Such is the attempt of love. That all such attempts are doomed to failure is not the point here. What is the point is that they all are placed by Sartre in the context of man's vain pursuit of being God.[22] Thus, it is clearly in this context that our ontological separateness (the first sense of conflict) and our mutual objectification (the second sense of conflict) give rise to conflict in the ordinary sense of the term. The fact that subjects other than me objectify me is a source of actual hostility because I want to be a being who is the complete foundation of its being. No doubt Sartre had this context in mind from the beginning, and that is why he used the term "conflict" as he did.

Let us now relate all this to Sartrean ethics. Since, according to the ontology, men necessarily desire to be God, this must mean, critics claim, that conflict in the overt sense of the term is inevitable in human relationships. Inasmuch as I want to be a being who would be its own foundation, I will always be upset (to use a mild word) by the fact that subjects ontologically distinct from me alienate my free subjectivity and give me a dimension of being that I cannot control. This will inevitably lead me into attempts to dominate and subjugate the other in some way. Of course, because he and I have the same basic desire to be God, conflict between us is inevitable. But if this is so, if Sartrean ontology has already determined the necessary character of relations among men, then it would appear that Warnock and others are correct in claiming that ethics, which attempts to say how men should and should not act towards each other, becomes unnecessary if not impossible.

B. SARTRE'S AND DE BEAUVOIR'S RESPONSES

This section is divided into two parts, each dealing with one of the objections presented in section A. I first consider at some length the charge that Sartrean ontology, since it considers human relations to be shot through with conflict, renders meaningless any moral obligation among men.

I presented above the various meanings of and contexts for the term "conflict" as used by Sartre. For ease of discussion it might be advisable to summarize them here. When he, in *Being and Nothingness*, speaks of conflict as inevitable in, and the basis of, human relations he refers to the following:

1. Ontologically, each individual is radically distinct from and the negation of every other individual. This ne-

gation is presupposed in all subsequent communal relations and can never be eliminated.

2. On the level of conscious experience, the original way I become aware of another as a subject is by becoming his (thinglike) object—and *vice versa*. Since all our subsequent relations, even those of a subject-to-subject type, are built upon this original one, they are rooted in an unavoidable "alienation" and "degradation" of our subjectivity that can never totally be overcome.

3. The third sense of conflict refers to attitudes that involve hostility and attempts at domination (love, hate, etc.). Such conflict is described by Sartre as occurring among men who are seriously attempting to be God and so are striving to overcome the frustration they experience because others objectify them.

Conflicts in senses 1 and 2 are inevitable because they are the very ground of human relations, according to Sartre. But, strictly speaking, in neither of them does conflict necessarily entail mutual hostility or attempts to dominate, destroy, or even hurt others (conflict in sense number 3)—though they apparently do tend in that direction. They do so tend because, he believes, there is in every man the basic desire to be God. And it is this context that critics have ignored. Sartre does *not* claim that all human relations involve hostility, but rather that such conflict is the necessary result when men try to use others to become God.

That harmonious relations between men are possible is affirmed by Sartre in a most significant footnote occurring at the end of his discussion of concrete human relations. This footnote states bluntly, "These considerations do not exclude the possibility of an ethics of deliverance and salvation." And it adds, "But this can be achieved only after a radical conversion which we cannot discuss here."[23] The references to ethics and to a radical conversion refer to his remarks about ethics at the end of *Being and Nothingness*, which have already been analyzed. The "conversion" is not to Marxism, as Warnock thinks; it is the choice Sartre discusses and encourages in the conclusion, the choice in which man ceases to take God as his supreme value and instead chooses freedom.[24] If I and another person cease trying to be God, we will cease in our attempts to abolish our alienating objectification and simply accept it as part of the human condition. We will accept the fact that we are ontologically distinct beings. Our relations, then, will not involve efforts at assimilation or destruction of the other's subjectivity with their ensuing conflict, for neither of us will try to eradicate, or become the foundation of, the objectivity the other confers on us. This will result in an ethics of "deliverance and salvation" (and Sartre repeats this very phrase in his conclusion) since it will free men from a life doomed to failure and from the inevitability of conflict rooted in attempts at destruction and/or assimilation of others. It will enable them mutually to support each other's freedom.

Men who choose to value their freedom in place of God, and who thereby choose to increase concretely this freedom in the world, will, Sartre says, simply accept the fact that there are many freedoms and that each is inevitably alienated and objectified by others. This is inescapable in a world peopled by many subjects. "To come into the world as a freedom confronting Others is to come into the world as alienable. If to will oneself free is to choose to be in this world confronting Others, then the one who wills himself such must will also the *passion* of his freedom."[25]

To repeat the point, though the conflicts of separation (number 1) and alienation (number 2) cannot be overcome, they can be softened if man stops trying to be God and simply accepts the inevitable objectification of his subjectivity by free subjects distinct from himself. Furthermore, these "conflicts" do not of themselves, as Sartre presents them, involve actual attempts to dominate or destroy others. The conflict that involves such attempts (number 3) is inevitable, according to Sartre, only if men refuse to accept their contingency—the presence in the world of other free subjects and the alienation caused by them. Since, as we saw in my chapter 2, he advises man to cease trying to fulfill his useless passion, this overt conflict is not absolutely inevitable, as are the first two.

The implication of all this as far as the ethics is concerned is, of course, that Sartre would deny that his ontology has rendered positive human relations impossible and moral obligations to undertake such relations meaningless. It remains true that his views in *Being and Nothingness* emphasize the negative. In his eyes men do tend toward actual hostility, basically because the other is always seen as a threat in terms of my desire to be God. But to claim that overt hostility is necessary and inevitable, would be, Sartre would say, to ignore the possibility of a radical conversion that would refuse to value that desire and its goal.

Even though positive human relations in some form may be possible in Sartre's ontology, we have yet to see why they are morally obligatory. More specifically, we have seen no justification for Sartre's statement in *Existentialism and Humanism:* "I am obliged to will the freedom of others at the same time as mine. I cannot make freedom my aim unless I make that of others equally my aim." It is time, then, to see what answers Sartre and de Beauvoir can give to those critics who claim that they offer woefully little to support this position.

From the start, it must be conceded that neither in his essay *Existentialism and Humanism* nor elsewhere does Sartre advance much to support his claim that a man is obliged to will the freedom of others. Only two short suggestions are put forth in that essay. Since they are so brief, it seems reasonable to analyze them and proceed immediately to point out their shortcomings, rather than saving the latter for the next section. We go on, then, to present other, better arguments offered by Sartre and, especially, Simone de Beauvoir.

The first suggestion Sartre offers centers around the notion of responsibility. Three years prior to this essay, responsibility had already been discussed at length in *Being and Nothingness.*[26] There he had emphasized that each individual through his choice confers meaning and value on the world and on other men. Inasmuch as an individual is the source of this meaning he is, of course, responsible for the value of others within his world—and it would be erroneous or attempted self-deceit for him to deny this. Still, it hardly follows that acceptance of this responsibility necessarily entails the decision to promote the freedom of other people. An individual could admit his responsibility for others and yet choose to value them as worms and move to enslave them. He would, of course, if he is honest, admit that he is responsible for that valuation and enslavement; but this is all that acceptance of his responsibility requires. Thus, responsibility in this sense does not establish the requirement for an individual to choose the freedom of others.

In *Existentialism and Humanism* Sartre advances a different aspect of responsibility. There he maintains that when a person chooses "he chooses for all men."[27] He explains that when a man acts in order to make himself the kind of person he wills to be, all his acts directed toward this goal create at the same time an image of man, an image of the way he believes man ought to be. In effect whatever a man chooses, Sartre claims, he proclaims it as a good, a value, not just for himself but for all men. It follows, he says, that in my choices and acts, "I am thus responsible for myself and for all men, and I am creating a certain image of man as I would have him be. In fashioning myself I fashion man."[28] If I choose freedom as the supreme value I will attempt to achieve, I am in effect affirming freedom as the supreme value or good for *all* men. I am in effect asserting that all men should become free. Note that Sartre is not just saying (in a somewhat Kantian vein) that when I choose a value I, at least implicitly, affirm that all men in a situation similar to mine in all relevant features should also choose this value. He is asserting much more. He is claiming that when I choose to become a certain type of person I propose as valuable an ideal (image) of what man should *be*, not simply what he should *choose*. When I choose my freedom, therefore, I am not thereby simply saying that all men should choose their freedom, I am proclaiming that all men should *be* free. I am implicitly asserting that freedom is a good for

79

all. The suggestion is that it would be inconsistent to assert this and then not will the freedom of all.

This argument, as Warnock notes, is in need of a number of qualifications and distinctions.[29] For one thing, it is necessary to distinguish, as Sartre does not, between a person's ultimate value and his secondary ones. It seems patently erroneous to affirm that in *every* choice of value I posit this value as a value for *all* men. The very most I proclaim is that my particular values are valuable for those men in situations similar to mine in all relevant respects. Only in the case of my ultimate value could it possibly be true that it is proposed as valuable for all men, for only in this case could my situation be similar to that of all men. What I mean is that the situation in reference to which the primary value of my existence is posited "could be" the human condition common to all men. I say "could be" in order to introduce another distinction. If my choice of my primary value is rooted in my conception of man—i.e., if my choice is of that which I believe to be valuable for myself insofar as I am human—then in effect I do propose it as a value for all who like me are human. On the other hand, if my choice of my ultimate value is based instead on what I consider valuable to me insofar as I am a unique individual, then, in my choice of it I would not be proposing it as a value for any other man. It appears that Sartre erroneously assumes that every choice of value, or at least every choice one makes of his primary value, is a choice of the first type—that is, a choice in which a person selects what is of value to him *as a man*, not simply as a *unique individual*.[30] To sum it up, Sartre's statement that when I choose I choose a value "for all men" is true only in the case of my primary value, and then only when my choice is based upon what I consider to be of value for me as a man, not as a unique individual.

Having thus sharpened Sartre's suggestion, we must now apply it to his argument for the choice of freedom as primary value. Since the argument rests upon his ontological view of man, especially his belief that human freedom is the source of all values, it is apparent that it is based upon a truth that he considers part of the universal human condition. Recall that the argument maintains that I should choose freedom as my primary value since it is in fact the source of all the meaning and value in my life. Since this fact—that the individual's freedom is the source of all the meaning and value in his life—holds true for all men, Sartre can legitimately claim that in my choice of my freedom as my primary value I in effect propose that each man's freedom should be his primary value. Since the basis for my choice of my freedom is a truth that holds for all men, I in effect assert that every man should make the same choice of his freedom that I make of mine. I propose, implicitly at least, an image of man as I would like him to be—namely, a man who asserts his freedom as his supreme goal, and so strives to become more and more free. I am responsible, then, for proclaiming this ideal as a value to and for all men. (And who would deny that an awareness of this responsibility could cause me anguish, as Sartre suggests?)

Still, even this notion of responsibility to others in no way demonstrates that I am obliged to choose as valuable anyone's freedom other than my own. All that the argument shows is that I am responsible for the image of man I project to others by my fundamental choice and corresponding acts. As for the choice of freedom, I am responsible for proposing as the primary value for each man his own individual freedom. But this is not to propose to any man that he choose to value the freedom of others. To proclaim that a man should accept and strive to increase his own freedom does not of itself demand that *I* accept or strive to increase his freedom, nor he mine. If Sartre wants to contend that it does, it is incumbent on him, then, to demonstrate that there is a necessary connection between my asserting that each man's freedom should be *his* supreme value, and my choosing his freedom as a value *for me*. Bernstein is correct; he simply has not done this.[31] Thus his contention that "I am obliged to will the freedom of others at the same time as mine" is not supported by his argument centered on responsibility.

We turn now to the second suggestion offered by Sartre

81

in *Existentialism and Humanism,* a suggestion based upon the interdependence of men's freedoms. He writes:

> And in thus willing freedom, we discover that it depends entirely upon the freedom of others and that the freedom of others depends upon our own. Obviously, freedom as the definition of a man does not depend upon others, but as soon as there is engagement I am obliged to will the freedom of others at the same time as mine.[32]

Unfortunately, no further explanation is forthcoming. Why does interdependence of freedoms mean I must will others' freedoms? Without a doubt, in the practical order my freedom is dependent on others' and theirs on mine. The range of options available for my choices and the power to attain the goals I seek depend on others. If I choose to increase my freedom, I should realize that this requires the assistance of others. Nevertheless, the fact that others are indispensable to me if I am to most effectively increase my freedom does not of itself demand that I choose to promote their freedom. In some situations it might be the case that I can most effectively increase my freedom by forcing others into my service. To compel others to serve me would not appear to be inconsistent with an admission of the interdependency of our freedoms. Indeed, it would appear to be a very logical response to this dependency. After all, all that consistency demands is that I choose *my own* freedom as my primary value. To see this, recall that Sartre argues that the choice of freedom is most consistent with the way things are, most consistent with the fact that freedom is the source of all values. Since it is only an individual's personal freedom that is the source of his values, this argument from consistency requires only that he choose his own freedom. Once again, no satisfactory support has been offered for the statement that "I am obliged to will the freedom of others at the same time as mine."

There is, however, another possible interpretation of what Sartre means by referring to the interdependence of men's freedoms. It may be that he does not mean the practical order, the area of action, but the order of knowledge. For earlier in *Existentialism and Humanism* he wrote, "I cannot obtain any truth whatsoever about myself, except through the mediation of another. The other is indispensable to my existence, and equally so to any knowledge I can have of myself."[33] Perhaps it is this dependency on others that Sartre has in mind in his reference to the interdependence of men's freedoms. Actually, the above passage is somewhat surprising coming as it does only two years after the publication of *Being and Nothingness*. In that work, even though he recognized that each man is known and therefore is given meaning by others, he insisted that such knowledge and meaning referred only to the "outside" of each person, to his being-for-others, not to his being as it is for himself.[34] As for his own self-awareness, Sartre spoke of it, even on a nonreflective level, as "lucid," "clear," "transparent," and "translucid." Thus, for example, it was impossible for a man to be unaware that he was free, even though he might not explicitly reflect on the fact, and that was why he tended to consider anyone who denied his freedom to be in bad faith. Furthermore, as far as the knowledge that others have of me is concerned, precisely because it is an *other's* knowledge of me, and because it is of me as an object not as a subject, Sartre maintained that it could not be directly grasped by me, though I could experience its presence. The objective characteristics that I have for others were said to be "unrealizable" and "unknowable" for myself. More importantly, he also insisted that the knowledge others have of me affects me only to the degree that I let it. I alone freely decide how I will "interiorize" the outside given me by the other.[35] Thus, the other's knowledge of me seemed quite inessential as far as my own awareness of myself was concerned. He never grasps me as a subject, nor can the objective meanings he gives me be realized by me, nor can they affect my own lucid self-awareness unless I let them. The other, Sartre wrote, "does not serve as a regulative or constitutive concept for the pieces of knowledge which I may have of myself."[36]

But if this is the case, how can the other be "indispensable" to any truth and knowledge I have of myself, as he claims in *Existentialism?* At the most he would be indispensable for me to have a vague awareness of my object side, my "outside." My lucid self-awareness certainly has no need of him.

I suggest that it is only in later works, the studies of Genet and Flaubert, as well as the *Critique of Dialectical Reason*,[37] that adequate explanation can be found for the position expressed in *Existentialism*. The fact is that Sartre has become increasingly aware of the tremendous influence of others not only over what we do but also over what we think, even over what we think of ourselves! As children, he points out, we first see ourselves through the eyes of others. We naturally adopt their view of the world and the identity they give us. Normally, there comes a time—adolescence—when the child challenges this identity and comes to realize that his own consciousness of himself as a subject is more certain than the meanings imposed on him by others. He comes to realize his freedom to accept or reject his object side. But for some this liberation never occurs. When children are subjected from their earliest days to great social pressure, Sartre says, they may from thenceforth ascribe more reality to what they are for others than to what they are for themselves. Genet, for example, became convinced as a child that in his innermost subjectivity he was evil precisely because society branded him a thief. He apparently could not even recognize his freedom to be something else. In the *Critique* and elsewhere, Sartre speaks of masses of people being "mystified" by their oppressors, so duped that they fail to realize their true needs and their freedom to reject the values imposed by others and to strive for their own goals. It seems clear that he now believes that the child as well as the adult who contains the child within him will not recognize his own subjectivity, not even his own freedom, if others do not acknowledge it. It is true that on one level, the prereflective, man can be aware of himself as a free subject without the help of others. But since as children we begin by taking the other's view of us as primary, we need verification from him before we will accept as true what our "inner sense" (our prereflective consciousness) reveals about ourselves. "Our certainty of ourselves finds its truth in the Other when the latter recognizes us."[38] Thus, we are dependent on others for our own self-knowledge; I attain truth about myself through the mediation of others. In terms of freedom, if others fail to acknowledge me as a free subject I will not reflectively recognize myself as free. My freedom is truly dependent on that of others.

Still, even if this is the type of interdependence of freedoms that Sartre is referring to in *Existentialism*, it is not clear why this would lead to the obligation "to will the freedom of others at the same time as mine." Even if others are indispensable to me if I am to know I am free, this does not require me to will their freedom. The master can learn of his freedom through the acknowledgment he receives from his slaves. In the absence of any further explanation by Sartre, we must wait until we see an argument of de Beauvoir's before the full significance of this interdependence of freedoms will be clear.

We leave *Existentialism and Humanism* at this point, for it has nothing more to offer in this matter. In only one other work does Sartre make even a brief suggestion to support his stated position. In *Anti-Semite and Jew*, written just after World War II, Sartre pleads for all to recognize that what befell the Jews can happen to any of us:

> Anti-Semitism is a problem that affects us all directly . . . if we do not respect the person of the Israelite, who will respect us? If we are conscious of these dangers . . . we shall begin to understand that we must fight for the Jew, no more and no less than for ourselves.[39]

His point seems to be that our only defense against being ourselves the victims of some arbitrary form of persecution is to join together to respect and fight for the freedom of all. No one will be really free, he adds, so long as a single person in the world is, or can be, oppressed.[40] For if any man is oppressed, I, who am no better (or worse) than he, may also be oppressed. Of course, what is implicit here is a belief in human equality. What is visited on one man or on a group of men can be visited on any, for no one can claim a privileged position in regard to others. Since all intrinsic or objective values have vanished in Sartre's ontology, no man can claim any ontological superiority over another. Inherently, we are in fact all equally valueless! Now, once I realize that I should in consistency choose to give primary value to my freedom, I can realize too that each person should do the same—and, as we saw above, I implicitly assert this in my choice. Since I also see that no man's freedom and values are intrinsically preferable to any other man's, I have no reason for preferring my freedom and values over anyone else's. Sartre seems to imply, then, that once this is realized I should choose everyone's freedom, not just my own. In the *Critique* he claims it is "contradictory" to recognize a man as a man, and then treat him as a dog.[41] In like manner, he may be saying here that it would be contradictory to recognize that all freedoms are equal and then choose to value only my own. This, in fact, is what some commentators interpret him to say.[42] This suggested argument, the best I have found in Sartre, has a certain force but ultimately is insufficient, I believe. However, I postpone criticism of it until section C.

A far more adequate argument, almost totally unknown by commentators, is offered by Simone de Beauvoir; I have found only one possible reference to it among them.[43] It includes the notions of equality and interdependency mentioned by Sartre. We have already pointed out that de Beauvoir accepts his ontology; that like him she maintains that only man creates value and meaning in this world. She also believes that all men seek meaning and justification for their existence. What follows, she argues, is a complete *interdependence* of man on man, for "Man can find a justification of his own existence only in the existence of other men."[44] I indicated in the previous chapter that each individual can give some justification (i.e., meaning) to his existence himself by personally choosing to value his freedom, but this needs qualification now. Not only does man want more than the solitary self-esteem of a single contingent being, he cannot even have self-esteem without others. As we pointed out above, man's self-knowledge is dependent on others. Man will not know he is free, let alone that he is justified, unless others acknowledge him as such. Of course, since man desires to be God he would like to give to himself the absolute justification for existence that a *causa sui* would possess. Lacking this, he would like to obtain justification from a being or beings possessing absolute value, de Beauvoir says. However, man is in a realm where the only sources of value are men, who are finite and intrinsically without value. Since only men can give my life meaning, since I will not even value myself unless they do, and finally since we desire as complete a meaning or justification for our existence as possible (including the most self-esteem possible), it follows that we want all sources of meaning, all men, to value our contingent existence.[45] If some refuse we will lack the meaning they could confer on us, and our self-esteem will suffer.

Because it is the other's freedom that is the source of his valuation of me, I must value his freedom if its valuation of me is to be significant to me. If I choose to deny any value to the other's freedom, I, at the same time, deprive myself of the ratification of my being that his freedom might offer me. Thus, I lessen the meaning my own existence can obtain, even in my own eyes. But to say I must *value* the other's freedom does not necessarily mean I must *promote* it. For even a man that I enslave can freely choose to give meaning to my existence, and it is not impossible for it to be a meaning involving respect and admiration. Thus, a master could value the limited freedom of choice of his slave and thereby value the meaning the obsequious slave freely confers on him. The master could truly value the slave's ability to create value—namely, his freedom—and at the same time not want to promote this freedom beyond certain limits.

Something must be added to the argument, then, if it is to establish my obligation to promote the freedom of other men. De Beauvoir adds the notion of *equality*. She observes that it is not the valuation of just any man that a person really desires. Man wants his life to be valued, to be judged meaningful, especially by those who can truly understand and appreciate it, by those who are his equals, his peers. What kind of self-esteem can the master really derive from the approval of slaves?

> The other can only accompany my transcendence if he is at the same point of the road as I. In order that our appeals [for meaning] are not lost in the void, it is necessary that there be near me men prepared to hear me; these men must be my equals [*pairs*].[46]

Recognition from a slave or a human robot is not what man ultimately desires. The self-esteem he gains from their approval is minimal. Though they can give some meaning to his contingent existence, it is hardly the degree or kind of meaning he cherishes. Man especially wants freely given approval from men able to appreciate his existence, those "at the same point of the road." Anything less is simply not enough to satisfy his quest for justification.

What this means, de Beauvoir argues, is that I must assist men to achieve the status of my equals. "I must then try to create for men situations in which they could accompany and surpass my transcendence. . . . I ask for health, knowledge, well-being, leisure for men so that their freedom is not consumed in fighting illness, ignorance, misery."[47] Obviously, if a man's freedom is consumed in fighting ignorance, etc., he will be unable to appreciate or give any positive value to those engaged in other pursuits.

Thus, de Beauvoir claims that it would be inconsistent with his desire for personal justification for a man to refuse to value the freedom of others and to prevent them from or not assist them in becoming his equals. Likewise, it would be inconsistent and self-defeating to attempt to *force* others to freely and positively value my existence. Such force will either provoke curses from him or, if I successfully control his freedom, he will not be able to give me the peer valuation that I most desire: "The man to whom I do violence is not my peer [*pair*] and I need men to be my peers."[48] If I want freely given respect and recognition from my equals, then, "I am only able to appeal to the freedom of the other, not constrain it."[49] In other words, "Respect for the freedom of the other is not an abstract rule: it is the first condition of the success of my effort,"[50] namely, to win the free approval of others and so attain justification for my life.

This is apparently meant to apply to *all* men. I must assist *all* men in becoming my peers so as to attain the maximum justification possible. If I can oppress or ignore "only one single man, in him all of humanity appears to me as pure things," she writes. Reaffirming the basic equality of all men, she adds, "if one man is an ant which one can crush without scruples, all men taken together are only an ant hill."[51] And if all men are only an ant hill, then, of course, any value they might confer on me would be insignificant to me. I should value and promote the freedom of all men because I want all to be my peers who value and support my existence. If I can deny the freedom of just one man, I in effect render meaningless that of all and so deny myself the justification I so deeply desire.

We have here the most complete argument offered by these existentialists to support their view that man should choose the freedom of others as well as his own. To sum it up—since God is dead, as are all objective values, man is completely dependent on the freedom of men if he is to attain meaning and value for his existence. Man fundamentally desires a justified existence and the knowledge that it is justified, and this means he wants to be freely and positively valued by all men, whom he wants to be his peers. Consistency demands, therefore, that man both value the freedom of all men and aid them in becoming his equals.

It is extremely important not to interpret this argument as a version of ethical egoism. It might be tempting to consider it to be based solely on self-interest, somewhat as follows. The reason I should promote the freedom of others is so that they will be my peers who can freely value and promote my freedom. But if that is the argument, then, what responsibility would I have to those who can never realistically become my peers or promote my freedom—for example, the retarded, those irremediably culturally disadvantaged, those who will never know me? The inescapable conclusion would be that I would have no obligation at all to such persons. It would be perfectly consistent with my desire for a meaningful existence to ignore, if not destroy, them, since any valuation I could receive from them, if indeed I could receive any, would be insignificant to me.

As I said, I do not think this interpretation of de Beauvoir's argument is accurate. When she states that I must "respect" the freedom of others, and when she speaks of my desire and need for "peer" evaluation, it seems clear that she is not advocating that I turn others into mere means for my own personal justification. If others become that, they simply would not be able to offer me the meaning and value I desire. As she points out, recognition from a slave or servant is not what man wants. In order to have any chance of obtaining the kind of justification for my life that I seek from other human beings, I must see them as my equals. I must see them as free beings, existing in their own right, as ends. "We are at one," de Beauvoir writes, "with the point of view of Christian charity . . . and Kantian moralism which treats each man as an end."[52] Only individuals whose freedoms I respect as ends in themselves could be my peers. Only they can give to my existence the kind of value affirmation that I crave.

It remains to spell out just what a choice to value and promote other people's freedoms means concretely, just how this choice is translatable into the social, political, and economic spheres, for example. This is done in the following chapters. In the remainder of this chapter I evaluate these responses of Sartre and de Beauvoir to their critics.

C. CRITICAL EVALUATION

I began this chapter by noting that Sartre himself has admitted his evolution from an individualistic concept of man to a greater awareness of his social dimension. I have also conceded to his critics that in *Being and Nothingness* he does accentuate the negative in human relationships. Granting all that, the fact remains that the status of social relations in Sartre is not nearly as bleak as his opponents claim. Very few of them have correctly noted the context in which he discusses these relations in that early work. Lack of close textual analysis has caused them to miss two essential points. First, in its initial usage the term "conflict" does not strictly mean actual hostility but ontological distinctness and psychological objectification, both of which may indeed cause men to tend toward overt hostility. Second, as far as conflict in the strict sense is concerned, Sartre does not claim that men as such are necessarily so related. He asserts that men who try to be God will inevitably attempt to dominate or be dominated by others. The radical conversion that he explicitly encourages (albeit in a footnote) indicates that men can cease trying to attain that unattainable God status, and, if they do, overt conflict among them can cease. Even their ontological separation and their mutual objectification will not be so threatening and sinister. Thus, in my opinion, even in *Being and Nothingness* Sartre clearly leaves open the possibility for human relations of a harmonious and positive kind.

The fact remains that he stresses the negative. That he does so is, I believe, because of two faulty premises, one of which I already criticized in chapter 2. As we saw, Sartre believes that men naturally tend to be in conflict because their basic desire to be the sole cause of the meaning of their existence (to be *causa sui*) comes up against the objectification given them by subjects separate from them. Since they cannot control or even directly grasp their objectification by others and since this objectification results in their being reduced to thinglike objects, they thereby cease to be free and to be the total cause of themselves. They are, therefore, naturally inclined to take measures to overcome this situation, which brings them into conflict with others who are doing the same thing. I have already said why I hesitate to accept Sartre's contention that all men naturally desire to be God. Fundamentally, I question whether experience shows that man wants to be totally free from meanings and values imposed on him by others, that he wants to be the sole cause of the meaning of his life.

I must also question Sartre's view of the nature of objectification of one subject by another. He much too facilely identifies objectification with reification, the reducing of a subject to a thinglike status. Of course, in one sense of the term, all knowledge of another subject objectifies it—where by objectify we mean "take as an object of knowledge." But Sartre means much more than this. For him, to objectify a subject is to grasp him as a thing and not as a free subject transcending his facticity. He offers no argument that this always takes place in face-to-face encounters. In fact, at times he seems to do little more than base his case on the term "objectification" itself, presuming that to know another as an object is inevitably to objectify, in the sense of reify, him. In other places, he relies on phenomenological analysis of various experiences to make his point; but since in *Being and Nothingness* it is only by and large negative experiences that he investigates, his conclusion is begged from the start. Surely, the phenomenological analyses of philosophers such as Marcel, Levinas, Scheler, and others, not to mention ordinary lived experiences of friendship and love, challenge his contention that face-to-face encounters between men inevitably result in reification of the subjects involved. The fact is, Sartre is quite cavalier in his treatment of this matter in *Being and Nothingness* and, in general, in his stress on the negativity of social relations.

I must, however, temper my criticism since I am convinced that he has changed his position somewhat. As we shall see in the next chapter, in the *Critique of Dialectical Reason* he no longer holds that objectification of a subject necessarily involves its thingification. Nevertheless, we shall find that in spite of a shift in his view of objectification, a definite negative perspective remains present in his conception of human relations even in this later work. And it continues to be grounded in his questionable belief that man desires to be God. More on this later.

Now, what about the reasoning Sartre and de Beauvoir offer to show that men should choose as their goal not just their own personal freedom but the freedom of all men? It is undeniable that Sartre offers at best the barest sketch of any arguments to support this. I have already pointed out the shortcomings of what he says in *Existentialism and Humanism*. The best suggestion he makes, in *Anti-Semite and Jew*, rests on the inherent equality of men. He implies that consistency demands that all freedoms be valued equally, since all men are equal inasmuch as no one possesses any ontological superiority over another—for all lack any intrinsic value. There is a certain plausibility to this proposal, but I see ultimately no reason to concede to Sartre that the equality of all men means that I must choose to value all freedoms equally. I see no contradiction in admitting on the one hand that all men are equal, that none possess intrinsic value, and yet choosing to value only my own freedom. To choose only my own freedom would not necessarily mean that I mistakenly, or in bad faith, consider it to be intrinsically more valuable. I could fully recognize that it possesses no intrinsic right to be singled out, and yet prefer it. Sartre himself would have to admit that by my very preference for it I do confer on it a value that no other freedom would possess. To choose to value something that possesses no intrinsic value over other things also lacking intrinsic value does not, I submit, involve inconsistency. Moreover, even though my freedom is not intrinsically superior, I do have reason for choosing it over others, the very reason we have advanced all along. My freedom and no one else's is the source of all my values and meaning. Thus, this suggested argument based on equality is, like all his other brief proposals, simply inadequate to establish my obligation to value the freedom of others.

On the other hand, de Beauvoir's argument found in *Pyrrhus et Cinéas* is far more satisfactory. It is noteworthy, as I mentioned above, that it appears to be almost totally ignored by commentators. Since man is completely dependent on the freedom of men if he is to attain any meaning or value for his existence and since he does fundamentally desire a meaningful existence, it follows that he needs to be freely and positively valued by his fellow-man. Furthermore, since he especially wants to be valued by free subjects who are his peers, consistency demands that he respect and promote the freedom of others. Only his peers, who can in their turn freely and positively value his existence, can give to him the kind of meaning and value he craves. I consider this to be a solid argument, especially since, as noted above, it is not intended to be a version of ethical egoism. There is a problem with it, however.

De Beauvoir certainly wants to demonstrate that I am obliged to value the freedom of *all* men. I suggested above that her remark, "if one man is an ant which one can crush without scruples, all men taken together are only an ant hill," is meant to show this. If I can ignore or destroy with impunity the freedom of just one man, then, she suggests, no man's or group of men's freedom will be significant to me since all men are of equal value intrinsically. However, this suggestion has dubious merit. Even de Beauvoir admits that it is my peers whose free valuation I most prize. Likewise, in the practical order some are of more value than others as far as the promotion of freedom for all is concerned. Is it true, as she claims, that man desires positive recognition from *all* men and, therefore, that he wants all to become his peers? Is it not rather the case that the good opinion of a select few is enough to satisfy him? Yes, I would be pleased if all men appreciated my life and work. I would like the plumber to value philosophy and myself as a teacher thereof, not to mention my colleagues in the sciences. But this is hardly a strong desire or need that I feel. For myself, and for most men, I suspect, it is a rather small peer group (plus those like their family for whom they are laboring) whose valuations they ardently court; the good opinion of all other men would be welcomed, but it is hardly a strongly felt need. Sartre himself has sought the favor of the Marxists more than that of anyone else. He has even disdained praise from the bourgeoisie; recall his refusal of the Nobel Prize. It may well be that man desires the most valuable life possible. It does not seem to be the case that this impels him to seek value from all mankind. If I am correct, then, it follows that no adequate reason has been offered by these existentialists for any man to respect or promote the freedom of a vast number on this planet, especially of those who never will know his name. I do not by this criticism mean to suggest that de Beauvoir for one is unaware of this difficulty,[53] nor that I believe other ethical systems have handled it better, but simply that her response to it is insufficient. It is no doubt a tribute to their humanity that neither she nor Sartre has let inadequate argumentation prevent them from spending their lives for the welfare of human beings who will never be able to offer thanks, let alone reciprocate.

In any case, whether they are able logically to justify it or not, Sartre and de Beauvoir do propose as their supreme value the freedom of all men. In the next chapter, I consider the positive side of human relationships in Sartre, specifically that relationship which he believes most effectively furthers the goal of freedom for all.

5

Freedom in the Group

Not only do Sartre and de Beauvoir proclaim the freedom of all men as the ultimate moral value, they also suggest how this goal is best realized. Sartre in particular describes the social relationship into which men should enter so as to most effectively promote the freedom of all, and both existential-ists offer general ideas on the form society as a whole should take. In my next chapter I present their understanding of the classless society. The bulk of this chapter analyzes what Sartre calls the "group," a relationship among men which he discusses at length in the *Critique of Dialectical Reason*.

I have no intention, by the way, of attempting the enormous task of determining the overall compatibility or incompatibility of this work with *Being and Nothingness*. Various authors have compared the two from different an-gles, and it appears that, depending on the perspective chosen, one can find items of similarity or points of disagree-ment. The two works are apparently compatible in some respects, incompatible in others. But such comparison is not really my concern. My intent is to show the compatibility between the Sartrean ethical ideal, freedom for all men, and the ideal human relationship presented in the *Critique*, the group. Not surprisingly, the union of men in the group is itself in some ways in agreement with his view of social relations in *Being and Nothingness,* and in others not. There is no question that in important respects Sartre has changed his conception of the nature of human relations, and I point this out in the appropriate places. Still, let me repeat, my primary interest here is not to compare positions of the *Critique* with those of the earlier work, but to demonstrate that the Sartrean moral ideal is in many ways effectively realized in the group.

A. Objections

We must clearly understand from the start that when Sartre speaks of the group he is not referring to just any collection of individuals. As an initial definition, let us describe it as a number of individuals consciously choosing to act together for common goals. They are acting as one and are aware that they are acting as one. Strictly speaking, the term "group" is first used to designate those relations that occur among individuals when they initially and spontaneously join together in the face of some menace and cooperatively strive to overcome their separateness and their inertia so as to better attain common goals.

In the *Critique* it is evident that Sartre believes that in this relationship man finds the possibility for the greatest enhancement of his freedom. In it men possess the most effective means of overcoming all obstacles to freedom, both natural and man-made. Thus, he calls the group in one of its forms "the origin of humanity," in which men are related as brothers.[1] Most important, it is described as "the free milieu of free human relations," and as such is said to be "the absolute end" of human relations.[2] For him to so designate it is clearly to identify it with his moral ideal, the freedom of all men. But this is where difficulties arise.

Many claim that the analysis Sartre presents of the relation of the individual to the group of which he is a member is such that the end result is "the suppression of individual liberty," rather than its enhancement.[3] No room remains in the group, they contend, for the free individual he so championed in his early works. Warnock, for example, believes that "the individual of *Being and Nothingness* has been swallowed up in the Group of the *Critique*."[4] Stack offers the same complaint; "the maturation of a group," he writes, "entails the negation of individual freedom in any true sense of the word." He continues, "The sovereignty of the group seems to entail the negation of individual freedom. The individual's praxis is entirely subject to the coercive power of the group."[5]

A similar criticism, from a slightly different angle, centers on Sartre's descriptions of the various stages in the dialectical evolution of the group, specifically its progressive deterioration into the rigidity of an institution and bureaucracy in which individual freedom is clearly subordinated to the collective entity. The point that the critics make is that, however humane and promotive of freedom the group may be in its initial stages, its regression into inert forms that suppress the individual is presented as inevitable. Thus Stack asserts:

> He [Sartre] describes dialectical processes as inevitable, proceeding from stage to stage in accordance with a necessity implicit in all social phenomena. . . . The free individual in a group inevitably is converted into the common individual and the common individual is ineluctably translated into an inorganic [i.e., unfree] being, a totality which the group uses for its own ends.[6]

And his conclusion is seconded by Warnock and Grene: "The social dialectic which is described in the *Critique* deprives man of as much freedom as does the dialectical method of the dogmatic Marxists. . . ."[7] Obviously, if these charges are true the group of the *Critique* can hardly be compatible with, or the realization of, his ethical ideal; and in spite of what he seems to say Sartre cannot identify them. Of course, to judge the validity of these interpretations, we must analyze in some detail his discussion of the relation between the individual and the group. This is done in section B.

Concluding this statement of objections, I present a different type of comment about the group, one frequently made by those who review Sartre's thought. They claim that the kind of human relationship he says is present there is simply impossible on the basis of the ontology of human relations set forth in *Being and Nothingness.* Sartre must have rejected that ontology, with its emphasis on conflict, it is said. I have already voiced some qualified agreement with this observation—qualified because I do not think that the change on his part is as radical as some suggest. In any case, in the sections that follow I indicate to what extent I believe he has modified his ontology in this area.

B. THE GROUP ACCORDING TO SARTRE

The notion of the group is developed at length only in the *Critique,* but it is prefigured to some degree in *Being and Nothingness* in Sartre's very brief discussion of the we-subject relation.[8] This relation, like that of the group, occurs when I and others act together for a common goal. In so acting I am aware that others are seeking this goal with me, and I am aware of them not as objects but as fellow subjects. There is no attempt at domination nor is there any reifying objectification within this relationship, and yet Sartre dismisses it as of little import. He does so because it in no way overcomes, and in fact presupposes, the irreducible separateness of individuals (conflict in the first sense discussed in *Being and Nothingness,* considered in chapter 4, section A). It is merely a "psychological" experience, not an ontological unity of subjects, he says. As a psychological experience, it involves only a "lateral" not a direct face-to-face awareness of others as subjects, which means the awareness that I have of them may not be shared by them. They may not notice me or our common action, and so no real unity of subjects would occur even consciously, let alone ontologically. Furthermore, Sartre points out, my lateral awareness of others as subjects presupposes a prior experience of myself as their object (conflict in the second sense discussed in *Being and Nothingness*, considered in chapter 4, section A), for only in that way do I initially experience them as subjects. Since it both presupposes and does not eliminate conflict in the senses of separateness and objectivity and since it does not involve a unity of subjects either ontologically or psychologically, the we-subject relation is a very secondary experience in Sartre's eyes. Its significance accordingly is minimized in his early work.[9]

Like the we-subject relation, the group of the *Critique* consists of many individuals acting as one for common goals. Unlike the we-subject experience, however, these individuals are aware that they are undertaking common actions and that they are within a group. As I mentioned earlier, the term "group" is first used to refer to the relation among individuals that occurs in the very first stage of their spontaneous joining together to overcome a common threat. One of the most obvious, but no less significant, characteristics of the members of a group is that they are not interrelated as antagonists, each a threat to the freedom and goals of the other, but as coactors cooperatively seeking mutually common objectives. It goes without saying that conflict in the sense of mutual hostility and attempts at domination (the third sense of conflict in *Being and Nothingness*, discussed in chapter 4, section A) is absent here, just as it was absent in the we-subject relation.

Let us note, however, in speaking of overt conflict, that in the *Critique* conflict in this sense is not said by Sartre to be based upon man's negative reaction to his objectification by others, as it was in *Being and Nothingness*; rather, it is rooted in the phenomena of scarcity, to a major extent at least. It is because of present scarcity (or fear of future scarcity) and the resulting competition for what is available that men fight.[10] Throughout history men have battled for the goods available. Those successful in attaining them have thereby been able to dominate the less successful, with the resulting alienation of the latter. And this term "alienation" has also changed in meaning, for here Sartre does not mean man's reifying objectification of man, as he did in his earlier work. He means, like Marx, man's impotence in the face of forces external to him, forces both human and nonhuman, even though he himself may have created some of these forces. The products men make, the embodiment of their work in matter, escape their control and come to dominate them; men, thus, become the product of their own product. This basically is their alienation.[11] (Indeed, in industrialized societies it is this alienation, not material scarcity, that is the problem for most men.)[12] In our day men are simply not in control of the complex socioeconomic dimensions of society, even though these dimensions originate in them. The mass of men is powerless in the face of inflation, pollution, unemployment, and bureaucracy. Alienation and conflict between men are rooted in scarcity, according to Sartre, and at times he gives the impression that that alone is responsible. However, there are also clear indications that the fact that the condition of men is, and has been, one of separation and isolation and the fact that men in general have not cooperatively united to fulfill their common needs are for him equally important reasons for hostility among them.[13] Men are, and have been, related (or, better, nonrelated) primarily as separate and distinct atoms, each attempting to fulfill his private needs. The result, of course, in a field of scarcity has been competition and conflict, and the eventual dominance of some over others. (And this does not seem all that different from the early work where ontological separateness tended toward conflict.) But if enough men joined into a common group pursuing the fulfillment of their common needs, scarcity might be abolished, Sartre indicates, and so too possibly the conflict based thereon.[14] His optimism about the possible eradication of scarcity seems to be based on the fact that men joined cooperatively in common action ("praxis" is the word he often prefers) simply have more power than they do when isolated. Together, they can most effectively combat their alienation—their dominance by forces external to them, including other men—though whether alienation in all its forms can ever be totally overcome is doubtful, as we shall see.

In any case it is clear that, insofar as the group enriches the power of the individuals within it, it increases their freedom. It increases this by being the most efficient way to deal with one root of hostility among men, and by enabling them to attain goals they could never achieve alone. We saw in chapter 3 that one of Sartre's meanings for freedom was the ability to attain goals, especially those goals which satisfy human needs. Certainly, fulfillment of human needs becomes more possible for men when they unite in a group with this fulfillment as their common goal. Sartre puts it this way: in the group men are able to cease being the product of their own product and become primarily their own product.[15] So far, at least, the group does indeed seem to be a most effective realization of the Sartrean moral ideal.

We should now move to confront directly the objections raised in the previous section, especially the accusation that the group in its internal structure entails "the suppression of individual liberty." We need to analyze in some depth the kind of unification that men in a group possess. This will involve two of Sartre's key notions about unification: that of the third party and that of "the same."

The function of the third party is to make manifest (Sartre uses the term "actualize") the lived unity of those with him within the group.[16] The third party is he who sees his fellow group members as undertaking actions that are the same as each other's and as his. Since each person in the group is the third in relation to all the others, each actualizes the unity of the others and is in turn himself unified with others by every other group member as third party. These overlapping internal unifications constitute the very unity of the group, according to Sartre.[17] This must be emphasized against those who claim that the individual is "swallowed up in the group." Group members, he insists, never constitute the substantial unity of a single organism. Their unity remains a practical one of common praxis; it is never an ontological oneness of some supraindividual entity. They are and never cease to be ontologically distinct individuals. Sartre insists on this so strongly that he is unwilling to admit that the group has a reality, even as a relational entity, which is more than simply the composite unity of its individual members.[18] And he also suggests that it is precisely because it can never become an ontological unity that it can never totally escape alienation (more on this later).[19] What exactly the ontological status of group unity is—a unity which is more than a mere collection of individuals and less than a supraindividual organism—is left unclear. It is clear that Sartre would maintain that he has not abandoned or obliterated the fundamental separateness in being of individuals that he so emphasized in *Being and Nothingness*. Yet it is also the case that in discussing the group he no longer stresses the negative implications of this ontological distinctness, and we must attempt to see why.

The notion of "the same" is central. What is especially significant about the unification performed by each third party is that his relationship to those whose unity he actualizes is not that of a subject to objects totally separate from himself. Though the members of a group are and remain distinct individuals, they are not separate as isolated atoms or as members of an inert series. They are unified in performing common actions for common goals. Thus each third party within the group does not see himself as other than and separate from objects whose unity he actualizes. Rather, he perceives his fellow members' actions as *the same* as his: "the practical unity which my totalisation reveals and which negates the objectivity of the group thereby negates my own in relation to the group, since this practical unity is *the same* (not in me *and* it, but *in us*)."[20]

Sartre admits that each third party as the actualizer of the group's unity can be said to be a "quasi-subject" in relation to those unified, who are correspondingly his "quasi-object." He grants, too, that the group unity actualized by a given third party cannot totally include that third party himself. He is quasi-transcendent, Sartre says, in relation to the group; he must be unified into it by other third parties. But the point is that this transcendence, these subject/object relations are only quasi-transcendence, only quasi-subjectivity and -objectivity. For they are the relations of those who act and see each other not as separate others or as objects but as *the same*. "Through the mediation of the group, he [my fellow member] is neither the Other nor identical (identical with *me*): but he comes to the group as I do; he is *the same* as me."[21] Because he is the same as me I find in his action not his Other-Being, Sartre says, but *my own* freedom, and he finds his freedom in my action.[22] "It is not that I am myself in the Other: it is that *in praxis* there is no *Other*, there are only several *myselves*."[23]

Thus, Sartre speaks of the group or, more precisely, of each member of the group as common third party, as "liquidating" seriality, and negating external otherness and the plurality of separate actions. Each third party interiorizes the multiplicity in seeing all acts as the same as his, with the result that his personal freedom is "synthetically enriched" and "swelled."[24] The fact that there are several myselves— we are numerically many and yet not isolated others—becomes, then, not a basis of conflict but an enrichment of our power, and so of our freedom. The more "myselves" there are, the more powerful I am: "number in *this* particular third party and in others does not appear as an *other-being* . . . but as the interiorised reality which multiplies individual effectiveness a hundredfold."[25] Plurality is no longer considered primarily as conflict or as potential conflict but as a positive enrichment of freedom, for it is the manyness of those who are not other than me but the same as me.

Though the group promotes man's freedom, it also, apparently, involves some limitations of the freedom of its members. It is this that the critics have fastened on. Insofar as I am in the group and want it to be effective, I must to some degree conform my action to that of my fellow members. The others as third parties become for me "regulating thirds," Sartre says. I cannot do whatever I please whenever I please, else the group as common action would be weakened, perhaps to the point of collapse. I must do those actions that together with the actions of others aid in achieving our common goals. Yet this limitation of my freedom is actually not the restriction it seems to be, he maintains. Again, the concept of the same is crucial. In the first place, my very presence in the group is freely chosen by me; I choose to act in union with others for common goals. But even more important, because all of us within the group are the *same*, in freely conforming my acts to their regulation I am in effect conforming to myself. The regulation of my acts is not by third parties who are others external to me. I follow their directions because I see them as mine. Thus, Sartre claims, their acts and directives involve no more limitation of my freedom than do my own, and he observes, "It would be absurd to suppose that an individual freedom could be limited *by itself* . . . .[26]

This notion of the same also results in probably the most significant advance of the *Critique* over *Being and Nothingness* in the field of human relations. In the former, unlike the latter, it is clear that to see another person as an object does not inevitably have as its result that he is simply degraded to the level of a thing. In the *Critique* objectification is no longer equivalent to the alienation of reification. We have already noted that alienation itself does not mean what it did earlier. In *Being and Nothingness* to objectify a subject was to reify it and so to alienate it. In the *Critique* alienation refers to the dominance of man by forces not under his control, and reification of man apparently has the same meaning.[27] Now, it is true that if a subject who objectifies me is simply an other, then, inasmuch as the objective dimension of my being is subject to his freedom, which is not under my control, this other could be said to alienate me. But in the group this situation does not obtain since my fellow group members are the *same* as me. In their freedom I see my own. Therefore, their quasi-objectification of me is not outside of my control; rather, "my objectification [by a third party who is the same as me] suddenly becomes my objectivity *for me*."[28]

Furthermore, such objectification as does occur among subjects in a group does not involve degradation to the thinglike level of the subjects objectified. Sartre stresses that within the group, since men grasp each other as *the same*, they see each other as free praxis, free subjects. Though they also see each other as objects (or quasi-objects), this objectification (or quasi-objectification) must, therefore, be of a much milder form than that which results in the reduction of a subject to a thing. It is worth noting that even in the simple relation of reciprocity in which two subjects mutually serve as means, and so as objects, for each other to attain their respective goals, even here objectification does not result in reification, according to Sartre. Though each inevitably objectifies the other, each at the same time recognizes that the other is a free praxis. Even though reciprocity involves a direct face-to-face relation of two subjects, Sartre does not hold, as he did in *Being and Nothingness*, that such an encounter inevitably objectifies at least one of the subjects involved, which becomes a reified object. In reciprocity each is both a subject and an object for the other; neither is seen simply as a thing.[29] Apparently, this is also the case for those in the group. They grasp each other as free subjects transcending any given facticity toward common goals, and as objects with a specifiable facticity. To repeat the point: inasmuch as in the group each sees his fellow member as the same free praxis as himself, the objectification that is present does not have as its result the degradation of the subject objectified to the status of a thing as it did in his early work.

Thus, in the group men recognize each other as free subjects and unite as such to achieve common objectives. No one is simply an other nor a reified subject. Certainly, a major reason the group is the most effective means an individual has of attaining the power to overcome obstacles to his freedom is that it consists in human relationships of a most positive type.

I have been speaking all along of the group as that social relationship in which Sartre in the *Critique* finds the possibility for the greatest enhancement of human freedom.

It is time to qualify this, for in fact it is not simply the group but the pledged group that is his ideal. The group can take either of two forms—the group in fusion (that is, one spontaneously arising in the face of some external threat), or the group consciously and deliberately formed by its members taking a common pledge to each other to maintain its existence. To illustrate, there is clearly a difference between a group of workers spontaneously striking for higher wages and these same workers subsequently forming together a more permanent body to carry on their fight. The latter would be a pledged group, which occurs when individuals of the original group in fusion attempt to prevent the group's dissolution by directly focusing their attention on the group and not simply on their common objectives, and by pledging to each other to keep it in existence. The group in either of its forms is an achievement of freedom, according to Sartre. But it is the group after the common pledge is given that he describes in most glowing terms as "the origin of humanity," in which men are related as brothers, and as "the victory of man as common freedom over seriality."[30]

Let us turn next to consider its structure. Doing so may enable us to discover how Sartre would respond to the second major criticism we set forth in section A. Recall that that objection claimed that however enhancive of freedom the group in its initial stage may be—and Warnock, for one, is willing to concede that it is—it cannot remain at that level. According to Sartre's portrayal of the movement of the dialectic, the group must evolve through stages of greater rigidity and inertia. It will eventually reach a point where individual freedom is totally alienated, because freedom is completely subservient to the institutional bureaucracy.

C. The Pledged Group

The pledged group is more highly praised than its predecessor because, unlike the spontaneous group, it involves a deliberate commitment of group members to each other.

The pledge is my guarantee and his that we will not become other, or separate from the group, but will remain within the group working for our common goals. In the group in fusion, though we work together for common goals, no commitment is made by anyone to perpetuate our communal relationship. Only by the pledge does each of us reflectively and deliberately give his free consent to the group relationship, and only by the pledge do we agree to maintain our praxis as common, as the same in each and all.[31]

Because the common pledge assures a greater permanence and unity in the group than is possible at its initial spontaneous level, Sartre considers the group after the pledge to have more *reality* than the group in fusion.[32] He insists that "the pledge is not a subjective or merely verbal determination: it is a real modification of the group by my regulatory action."[33] This "real modification," which he goes on to call our "common-being," is the creation of a "new entity," "man as a common individual."[34] (It is this creation that he calls "the origin of humanity.") Yet these phrases, "common-being," "new entity," "common individual," should not be taken to mean that all those within the pledged group literally merge into a single individual or superorganism. Sartre continues to insist that such is not the case, and states that *"our common being . . . is a mediated reciprocity of conditioning."*[35] That is, we have a "common" being not because we literally become the same substance but because we each take the same pledge to each other that our actions will be conditioned by those of others so as to maintain common action for our common goals. We remain ontologically distinct individuals sharing a common commitment to each other. Thus, Sartre says, our being is common because we recognize each other not as others but as "accomplices" in the common act that removes us from the slime of seriality. In another group member I see "my brother whose existence *is not other than mine.*" Again, this does not mean we are literally one being, for, he adds, we are brothers not because of physical resemblance or an identity of nature but because "following the creative act of the pledge, we *are our own sons*, our common creation."[36] Our brotherhood consists not in substantial oneness but in a mutual bond formed by our common pledge. And he suggests that relations such as friendship, comradeship, and love are simply further free specifications of this basic fraternity existing among those who take the same pledge.

It seems clear that it is precisely this fraternal relationship that Sartre and de Beauvoir think should exist among authentic individuals who freely choose the freedom of all men. This is not to say that every pledged group, nor every group in fusion for that matter, is equivalent to a group of men freely choosing the freedom of all. Obviously, any group can have goals other than freedom—a group of Kamikazi pilots, for example. But in order for men to effectively fulfill their obligation to choose the freedom of all in the long run, they need to commit (pledge) themselves to maintain in existence social relationships involving mutual cooperation and common actions to promote their common freedom. In the previous chapter I pointed out that both Sartre and de Beauvoir stress the interdependency of human freedoms, the latter arguing that the only consistent way for a man to relate to others so that they will freely choose to value and promote his freedom is for him to choose to value and assist them in promoting theirs. The ideal, then, would be that all men commit themselves to doing just this, which is to say that they form a pledged group and become brothers seeking the freedom of all.

Though the pledged group represents a victory of freedom and is the most effective means of promoting freedom in the long haul, Sartre acknowledges that it too contains limitations of freedom, even more limitations than the group in fusion. The reason for this is that the pledged group involves explicit reflection on itself; it takes itself as its object, while the spontaneous group does not. In the latter each person concentrates his attention on the common objective, not on his fellow member. The awareness those in that group have of each other is thus only lateral,[37] which is another reason why Sartre speaks of them as quasi-subjects and quasi-objects. In order to make the group permanent, we reflectively focus our attention on it; we explicitly make each other objects, not just quasi-objects. The result is there is more otherness, more "distance," between myself and my fellow group members.[38] However, this does not mean that we see each other as reified subjects, nor that we return to a serial condition of simple separation, for we are still "the same" and see ourselves as such. We are, Sartre admits, Other-Beings but, "We do not relapse into seriality, since, for each third party, this *Other-Being* is *the same* Other-Being as for his neighbour."[39] Nevertheless, there is apparently less sameness here than in the group in fusion, and for this reason he locates the pledged group between it and the simple otherness of serial relations.[40]

Because there is more otherness in the group after the pledge, regulations that come to my freedom from other third parties within the group are seen as greater limitations than was the case in the spontaneous group. In the latter we so identify with each other that the directives to me from another third party are directives to me from myself. In the pledged group this degree of sameness is not present. The third party who regulates my freedom is not simply the same as me (though he is that); he is explicitly seen as other. Insofar as it is he as other that limits my freedom the limitation is not from myself and so is to some degree a restriction of my freedom.[41]

The limitations of freedom present in the pledged group are also manifest in Sartre's notions of obligation and terror. *Formal* obligations to those in the group arise only when a pledge has been given to them. Strictly speaking, an individual in a spontaneous group has no obligation to anyone to remain in that group since he has made no commitment to do so. If he leaves he will, of course, become more vulnerable to external threats, which the group arose to combat. However, once he has pledged to remain in the group he has a formal obligation to do so. If he were now to leave, he would be vulnerable not only to an external threat but to one from within the group itself. Through his pledge to others in the group, he gives them the right to discipline and even liquidate him if he fails to remain in the group. This internal threat of violence Sartre calls terror, and he claims that it is not primarily a destructive but a "cohesive" force in the group. It is the fear of this terror that keeps all permanently within the group, even when external threats have subsided. It is a source of unity also because in making the same pledge all members of the group are subject to the same terror. Those to whom I have obligations, those to whom I am subject in terror, are still the same as me, granted that this sameness is less than in the group's earlier stage. Even as he objectifies me, and I him; even as he obliges me, threatens me, or kills me, and I him—he remains, Sartre says, a "brother, whose existence *is not other than mine.*"[42] Nevertheless, the very presence of obligations and of this terror clearly involves more restrictions of freedom than were present in the spontaneous group. I am less free to leave the group or to deviate from its common praxis after my pledge.

Of course, in the final analysis the whole purpose of such restrictions is to ensure the unity and existence of the most effective means of human liberation and fulfillment. Whatever restrictions are present are freely chosen by me in my pledge and are imposed on me by others, who are to a great degree still the same as me and seen as such. On balance the pledged group, according to Sartre, is an instrument for the enhancement, not the limitation, of my freedom. Even though it contains greater restrictions of freedom than does the group in fusion, these very restrictions result in its being more effective for the long-term promotion of freedom. My becoming the object of others in the group and they of me, our reciprocal obligations, our common subjection to terror, all of these are necessary to ensure the group's permanence. The problem is that once men have turned their attention to the reality of the group itself and have taken steps (initially through the pledge) to ensure its continuation, there is danger that the inertia given to the group will be made stronger and stronger and that the group, therefore, will evolve into collectivities in which inertia predominates over freedom. In the *Critique* Sartre describes in detail such a process—the spontaneous rising of a group from seriality, its permanence established by the pledge, and then its progressive deterioration into an institution and bureaucracy, and eventually its return to the series. In some of the most pessimistic sections of this work, he portrays this deterioration as inevitable: "groups have a serial destiny even in the moment of their practical totalisation."[43]

I do not attempt to review the detail of his analysis. Suffice it to note that what happens is that as the reality of the group is more and more focused upon, as its unity and permanence become its primary objective, individual freedom becomes more and more suspect. Because the individual in his freedom is always able to leave the group or deviate from its norms, and hence weaken or even destroy it, because he is never totally integrated into it as into a supraindividual organism, but remains quasi-transcendent, increasingly stronger attempts are made to ensure his permanent status within the group. The result is that his freedom becomes more restricted. Eventually, the only freedom left to the individual is the freedom of the collective, Sartre states. At the same time, since it is the reality of the collective that is paramount, not that of any particular member, each individual as such gradually becomes expendable. Only his task or function within the collective is considered essential. What is taking place in effect is that the collective is attempting to make itself a true ontological unity, to be not just a unity of action, so as to guarantee its existence. It is trying, ultimately without success, to merge free individuals into one overarching organism.[44]

Is this devolution of the group to a bureaucracy and series inevitable, as the critics claim? Certainly, the *Critique* can be interpreted as saying so. Yet in recent interviews Sartre has suggested the possibility of a group remaining in its initial group status.[45] And there are some indications in the *Critique* itself that he considers that a possibility even there.

The issue is especially complicated by the fact that Sartre maintains that the dialectical movement of human history is necessary.[46] I confess that I am not altogether clear about his use of this term, but the following interpretation seems plausible. He does deny that the kind of necessity involved is that of "constraint," meaning exterior forces opposing themselves to free praxis. The necessity in the dialectical movement is rather defined phenomenologically as the experience "of a retroactive power eroding my freedom . . . but nevertheless emerging from it."[47] When I freely act on the world, he explains, the result of my praxis *inevitably* takes on a life of its own to some degree. Because I do something to beings (whether things or men) external to me, what occurs as a consequence of my action on them is partly outside of my control. Necessity is "the *destiny in exteriority of freedom.*"[48] Things happen as a result of my free action that I did not directly intend or want and that I could not prevent. Yet, and this is crucial, these results are the consequence of my free action. Now, the kind of necessity he refers to here is certainly not of a logical type, where conclusions are rigorously deduced from premises. Nor does it seem to be of a strictly mechanical type, where events are connected in rigid chains of causality. This necessity is said to emerge from human freedom, and I take that to mean that, because I freely decide to do certain things, certain other unintended, and maybe unwanted, results inevitably follow. Because men freely decide to cut down trees, one inevitable result will be the erosion of the soil. But suppose a different decision had been made and a different action undertaken? Then, of course, a different result inevitably would have occurred. It seems, then, that the necessity proposed here is of a hypothetical kind; if I decide to do A, B inevitably will occur as well.

To apply this to the analysis of the group, we could say, following Sartre's notion of necessity, that if men in the group in fusion decide to take the pledge a certain rigidity will inevitably be introduced into their relationship. But, of course, men may freely decide not to pledge, and then, I suppose, the spontaneous group will inevitably dissolve. Now, if men do choose to pledge to maintain the group's existence, does Sartre mean to say that the necessary result in the long run will be the institution and the eventual dissolution into the series? If my interpretation of his notion of necessity is correct, the answer is no. The deterioration of the group into a bureaucracy and series inevitably takes place because the permanence of the collective itself is taken as an end and comes to be more important than the free development of the individuals who form it. But if the group took as its primary goal from the beginning the freedom of each of its members, that unhappy consequence would not occur. Indeed, freedom was the group's goal initially, Sartre notes, for it arose out of the need to free man from alienation—his dominance by forces external to himself. The original goal was to make man his own product rather than the product of such forces.[49] In the *Critique* he portrays what happens when this is forgotten and the reality of the group itself becomes primary.

Thus, as I interpret him, the devolution of the group need not take place. On the other hand, it is probably true that in Sartre's eyes men have a natural tendency to seek to ontologize it, rooted in their natural desire to be God. To strive to make the group into a permanent being is to attempt to do on the social level what men attempt to do on a personal level—namely, to achieve for themselves such permanence and necessity in being that their existence is assured. They would exist, then, by right, not by chance. Once they recognize that neither socially nor privately can they become self-necessitating substantial beings, men can undergo a radical conversion *on both levels*. They can individually reject being God as their personal goal and choose freedom instead. Collectively, they can cease to attempt to turn the group into a substantial organism and instead take their communal freedom as their common goal. In doing so the group of free individuals does exactly what Sartre himself suggests. "It posits itself for itself . . . as the free milieu of free human relations." And it is just such a pledged group taking freedom as its goal that, he claims, "is both the most effective *means* of controlling the surrounding materiality in the context of scarcity and *the absolute end* as pure freedom liberating man from alterity [i.e., separate otherness]."[50] Obviously, it is precisely such a group—the free milieu of free human relations, the absolute end—that is to be sought by those individuals who choose his supreme value, the freedom of all men.

D. CRITICAL EVALUATION

At the beginning of this chapter I stated that my intent was to show the compatibility between the Sartrean ethical ideal, freedom for all men, and the ideal human relationship presented in the *Critique of Dialectical Reason*, the group. I consider this accomplished. As we have seen, Sartre himself unequivocally asserts that the group in its early stages is for him the "free milieu of free human relations" and the "absolute end as pure freedom liberating men from alterity."[51] Contrary to what some claim, the group as spontaneous and pledged does not obliterate or "swallow up" individual freedom. For one thing, as we saw, Sartre insists that even after the mutual pledge it never becomes an ontological or organic unit absorbing its members. It remains a practical unity of conscious action, interwoven praxes, which is to say it is a unity of, and rooted in, the free decisions and actions of those who join it. In spite of the fact that he grants more reality to the pledged group, Sartre continually returns to this theme—the group in any form is nothing but common praxis. Even when it takes itself for its object it becomes no more than "frozen," or preserved, common praxis.[52] In fact, the ontological separateness of the group members is so dominant in his mind that only fear (terror) can hold them together, and even then the unity is not a oneness of being. Furthermore, though the individuals who choose to remain in the group cannot do just anything they please because their actions must conform to each other, this freely chosen limitation is not mainly a restriction of freedom. In the first place, as Sartre points out, since such limitations occur among men who freely identify with each other (they are *the same*), they are in effect placed on me by myself. To consider them simply as coercive of my freedom would be inappropriate. If a man freely decides to act cooperatively with others and so limits himself to doing x rather than y (and all actions involve such limitations; one can never do everything all at once), in his doing x he is doing precisely what he chooses to do. To call this self-limitation coercive or a lessening of his freedom would be nonsense. Moreover, since his free presence in the group is a means for him to achieve degrees of human fulfillment unattainable alone, and since he naturally desires this fulfillment, in this respect too the group enhances rather than squelches his freedom. It enables him to more effectively attain what he naturally seeks.

It is true that the exact ontological status of the group remains obscure. Though Sartre clearly says that it never becomes a supraindividual reality but remains a unity of actions, at the same time he claims that group praxis is not merely a collection of individual praxes but something more —a "synthetic enrichment" of individual praxis—and he agrees that the intelligibility of the group is more than that of all the individuals within it.[53] He seems unaware that to admit the whole (the group) is more than the sum of its parts (the individuals in the group) is to give it some kind of extraindividual reality. A similar point could be made about his concept of "the same," which plays such a central role in his attempt to explain the unity of the members of the group and still preserve their individuality. The unity of the group is one of sameness, though not one of identity in being. Again he fails to realize that to admit the reality of sameness is to posit a unity in being not totally reducible to the reality of a plurality of individuals. As others have suggested, what his dialectical "nominalism" lacks is a thoroughgoing ontology of relations.[54] Be this as it may, even if the group does possess more ontological reality than he is willing to admit, it seems to me that in its initial phases, before its permanence has become the dominant concern of its members, it is certainly inaccurate to describe it as "the negation of individual freedom."[55]

As for the other charge, that the group cannot remain in its initial phases, I concede that the issue is far less clear. As I noted above, it seems that in recent interviews Sartre has spoken of the group remaining in its original stage. I have attempted in section C to square such remarks with his account of its devolution into the institution and the series. If my interpretation of his notion of necessity and my emphasis on those few pages where he suggests that another fate is possible are correct, then his critics are wrong. But I admit that the turgid style of the *Critique* leaves me less than certain that my reading is accurate. It may be that in light of his recent remarks one should simply admit that he has changed his mind since he wrote the *Critique*. In any case it appears that he *now* believes that a group can remain in its pledged form.

There is at least one area in which he most probably has changed his estimation of the group. Though he still believes the pledged group is the "most effective means" to overcome alienation, it is extremely unlikely that he considers it today to be the "absolute end" of human relations. The relations of men within groups involve lessening or eliminating conflict, positive cooperation and fraternity, unity, and even subject to subject (or, more accurately, subject/object to subject/object) relations. But, as we have seen, the unity of these subjects is a practical one of action; it occurs insofar as they act together for a common goal. Two or more individuals, friends, simply delighting in each other's presence and having no goal other than the mutual sharing of each other's being, do not, therefore, appear to be what Sartre would call a group. Perhaps non–action-oriented relations of friendship could fit under his ideal "free milieu of free human relations," but I am dubious. For in the *Critique* this milieu is described as a pledged group; and, since group means a unity of common praxis working for a common goal, it would seem rather odd to describe men simply delighting in the free sharing of each other's being as a group in any sense.

Actually, in some very recent interviews Sartre shows that he is clearly aware of the difference between a relationship that is totally practical in character and friendship, "a relation which surpasses the action undertaken."[56] He complains that the Communist party, for example, does not value the latter and so discards individuals when they cease to have practical value. And he leaves no doubt that his present ideal of human relations includes kindness, respect, and love, none of which he reduces to common action.[57] Love, for instance, is the acceptance of the total person, and not of just that part of him having practical value. For this reason I believe that the group of the *Critique* is no longer Sartre's final word, no longer the "absolute end," when it comes to human relations. Unfortunately, he has written next to nothing to explain these human relations that are more than united praxis. No reason has been offered for his shift from his statement in the *Critique* that love, friendship, etc., are rooted in common action, and so are simply further specifications of the relations of individuals unified by terror into a pledged group, to his recent opinion that they are relations that surpass common action and are not reducible to it. Nor is there any indication that he realizes how far he has moved beyond the *Critique.*

Another difficulty arises if we compare recent statements with those in the *Critique* that fear and terror have a central role in maintaining the unity of the group. Recall that terror was necessary, Sartre said in the *Critique,* to preserve the permanence in existence of the pledged group. But it seems incredible to assert that a community united in love and friendship must be held together by fear and terror. I presume that Sartre would not say this now. In fact, in other post-*Critique* works, he even speaks of the group itself as eliminating all thought that would conceive of one's fellow-man as antagonistic to, or even indifferent to, him and his goals. Precisely because it overcomes the atomic individualism that separates man from man, racism, sexism, and class distinctions disappear in the unity of the group, he says.[58] But if that is the case, why is terror so necessary in the *Critique* to keep men cooperatively working together? Why did he consider the unity of the group to be so fragile that only fear could force men to remain in it? Why could they not join together out of love, particularly if the group eliminates all conceptions of the other as an antagonist? I suggest the reason is that in the *Critique*, though he has moved some distance from the overemphasized individuality of *Being and Nothingness*, Sartre still views men as so individualistic, so separate, so fearful of the loss of their personal freedom that they cannot continue to cooperate and unite with each other over a long period of time. That is why the threat of violence is necessary. That is also why the group ultimately tends to dissolve into seriality, no matter how harsh the steps taken to prevent it. And it explains why he remains undecided whether the abolition of scarcity really would remove all hostility between men. Recent statements about love, friendship, and group unity eliminating all antagonism and indifference indicate he has moved toward a more positive and, in my opinion, more adequate understanding of human relations. But the absence of any clear change in the philosophical underpinnings of his concept of social relations leaves this move and his new views unaccounted for. I am certain that no matter what else he might now believe about them, friendship and love do not involve subjects literally sharing each other's being. Sartre's opposition to any supra-individual monism remains constant, I suspect, just as it was constant from *Being and Nothingness* to the *Critique*.

I did refer just now, however, to some changes in Sartre's views, or at least changes in emphasis, from one work to the other. I conclude this evaluation by indicating points of difference and points of constancy, as far as human relations are concerned. Many of these have already been noted in sections B and C. Even so, it would be worthwhile to collect all those scattered remarks here.

First, let us remind ourselves, lest the differences between these books be taken as more significant than they are, that even in the early work Sartre opened up the possibility of positive, harmonious human relations. The we-subject relation was, of course, of this type; and, as we saw at length in the preceding chapter, overt hostility and conflict among men could be eliminated if they underwent a radical conversion. Thus, the fact that within the group men are not in actual conflict with each other is not in principle a radical change from *Being and Nothingness*. It allowed such relationships—it even had one in the we-subject—though admittedly it barely mentioned them. Never forget that Sartre himself has said that in that work he was basically analyzing men of bad faith—those individuals who had not made a radical conversion, which would have meant choosing freedom rather than being God as their primary value.[59] Certainly, in the *Critique*, at least as far as the analyses of the spontaneous and pledged groups are concerned, his focus is different.

Another clear difference, also noted above, is the change in his definition of the term "alienation." It no longer means simply objectification by another, but dominance by forces outside of one's control. Even more significantly, as we stressed earlier, Sartre no longer claims that objectification of one subject by another inevitably means a reduction to a thinglike status of that subject. (Recall that objectification itself was called a type of conflict in the early work.) I can grasp another subject as an object (or quasi-object) in the group, and because of our mutual identification (we are *the same*) this objectification does not reify him. He further clearly indicates that subject to object or object to subject relations are not the only possibilities for two individuals who directly confront each other. In the group, and even in relations of reciprocity, subject/object to subject/object relations are possible. Note, by the way, that he never states that pure subject to subject relations are attainable in direct face-to-face encounters. Though in such instances I do see others as subjects, I also view them as objects. Even in the spontaneous group, where the attention of all is focused on some third entity as the common object, the members relate to each other not as pure subjects but also as *quasi-objects*.

Apparently, this means that some kind of objectivity is always present in our consciousness of others, even when we primarily view them as subjects like ourselves, and I would agree.

Another important difference between the two works is the way Sartre looks at ontological plurality. In *Being and Nothingness* the fact that there were many other subjects distinct from me was a threat to me—he used the term "conflict" to highlight this. In the *Critique* the plurality of others, who in the group with me are "the same" as me, is a positive enhancement of my freedom, he says. Still, even there, the ontological separation of man from man continues to pose a problem for Sartre. This ties in with what I said earlier. Even in the later work he views men as too individualistic, too distinct, and too fearful of losing their freedom to be able to unite permanently in cooperation with others. Only violence can keep them together, and even it cannot prevent the tendency of the group to return ultimately to seriality. The difficulty is in the way Sartre views men's ontological distinctness, not simply in the fact that men are separate individuals. He sees men as separate beings, who tend to remain so. They do not naturally incline to join together to share their freedoms, their very lives, for any length of time. Each man is so jealous of his personal freedom that he is fearful that uniting with others, no matter how benevolent they are, will result in its decrease.[60] As we have said time and again, Sartre looks at man this way because he believes that he naturally desires to be God, to create for himself permanence and stability in being by giving himself the meaning and justification for his existence. Even if man, after a radical conversion, refuses to value this useless passion and its unattainable goal, the basic desire to be a self-cause remains. No matter how authentic he is, therefore, he will have a deep-rooted tendency to see others as inimical to his freedom.

This also explains Sartre's hesitation in the *Critique* when it comes to the question of the abolition of conflict among men. Frequently in that work he suggests that scarcity is the source of conflict and that the abolition of it will eliminate hostility. At the same time, he admits to being undecided whether alienation of man by man can be totally abolished even in an ideal community.[61] For even there, he says, men will remain ontologically separate, and might not this very separateness provoke conflict? Indeed it can, and recently he has conceded that antagonism among men will exist even when material scarcity is abolished.[62] Even if all men had enough to satisfy their basic material needs, there is no guarantee that some might not choose to prey on others. This would remain a possibility because men are free individuals who can never join in an ontological unity and especially because men are naturally suspicious of the meanings others give them and naturally fearful of losing their freedom if they allow others to be free. Scarcity no doubt plays a significant role in promoting conflict, but it alone is not the root of man's inhumanity to man in Sartrean ontology.

I have already taken issue with Sartre's belief that men desire to be God, and my criticisms are not repeated here. Suffice it to say, no matter how much he has changed since he wrote *Being and Nothingness*, he continues to have an overly individualistic view of man, which has adverse effects on his understanding of genuine human community. Relationships based on love and trust rather than fear and practical advantage remain unexplained, and are perhaps unexplainable. He is still a long way from grasping Aristotle's naturally social man. This is not to deny that Sartrean man has need of others. He certainly does if he is to promote his freedom effectively and maximize the love and meaning he may obtain in his life. Yet in the *Critique* these social needs are sufficient only to induce men to join together spontaneously when conditions are right to combat some external threat. These needs are not enough to keep them working cooperatively for long-range goals, even when these goals involve their mutual well-being. For this, violence is necessary. As Warnock correctly observes, this perspective on human relations remains closer to that of Hobbes than to that of Aristotle[63]—let alone to the I-Thou relation of Marcel and Buber!

6

Freedom and the Classless Society

In section A of this final chapter, I indicate in general what the "free milieu of free human relations" becomes in the political realm for Sartre. I also discuss the specific moral norms that have been derived by him from his supreme value, freedom. In section B, I offer my final evaluation of Sartrean ethics.

A. The Classless Society

I have no intention of going into detail on the many and varied political stances Sartre and de Beauvoir have taken over the years. Many others have already done this well.[1] Rather, I indicate the general type of political structure Sartre finds most compatible with his moral and social ideal. In the process we see that it is not the case that his espousal of Marx's ideal society has meant a wholesale rejection of his early positions on freedom.

It would be good from the start to remind ourselves of some of the points made in chapter 1 of this book, where Sartre's intellectual development was discussed. We noted that since the student rebellion of 1968 he has come to believe that the intellectual must take his cue from the masses and serve them by articulating their desires, needs, and goals. He must not attempt to define their needs and goals for them nor go to them with ready-made programs that he expects them to implement. He now claims that the only way to achieve a free society for all men is by forging a direct relation with those who demand such a universal society, the masses. I repeat all this because it helps to explain his reluctance to offer specific directives on how to attain his society of freedom. It also explains why he is vague as to what exactly this ideal society would be. Apparently, its precise nature and the ways to attain it must be determined by those who most need and desire it, those most alienated. Add to this Sartre's own admission of incompetence on the level of technical political action,[2] and we should be further dissuaded from expecting specific proposals from him. Finally, he has asserted more than once that it is ridiculous to think that those like us who live in a world dominated by scarcity, oppression, and alienation could conceive in any detail what the ideal free society would be.[3] At the most we can have some general idea of its structure, and this is what he does offer.

As is well known, Sartre's ideal society is Marx's classless society. We need to show why the free milieu of free human relations turns out to be identical with Marx's ideal. One of the central reasons for this is that a classless society would not have the domination of one group by another that occurs in capitalism and in many forms of socialism. Class structure in Sartre's eyes inevitably implies inequality and domination of some by others. In a classless society all would be equal, all would be peers. It would be composed of men who in de Beauvoir's eyes could best offer and attain justification for their existence (see above, chapter 3). In it all would equally participate in the governance of the society. The State, meaning an elite ruling class, would be abolished. In his *Critique* Sartre attacks the tremendous bureaucratization and centralization of power in both capitalism and socialism. He argues for "debureaucratization, decentralization, and democratization" and calls upon the sovereign group or class to relinquish its monopoly on society.[4] What he wants is a *direct* democracy, one in which all people participate in self-governance. His ideal is that the masses unite into a pledged group, for only then, and not simply through the ballot, can their wishes be expressed effectively. Even if a direct democracy needs to take a representational form, Sartre argues for a new system in which, for example, a representative elected by 5000 people would "be nothing other than 5000 persons; he must find the means to himself be these 5000 persons."[5] One might wonder if it is practical or even possible to find such means; nevertheless, his intent is clear enough. All men must be in control of their political institutions. Direct democracy is also advocated in the economic realm. Since he accepts the Marxist position that political superstructures are rooted in an economic base as their substructure, he, like Marx, demands also that the alienated masses attain control through collective ownership and management of the instruments of labor.[6] He approves of groups of workers collectively managing their factories and, I might add, of students together with faculty and administration running universities. Exactly how this is to be implemented in practice remains unspecified.

A direct democracy, as Sartre views it, would be the concrete embodiment of a free society of free individuals mutually choosing to promote each other's freedom. In it all men in the society would be able to participate freely in shaping their destiny. In it all men join together (in a pledged group) to select the goals that they believe will fulfill their mutual needs. Respect for the freedom of all is present, for no man's free choice or vote is considered to be superior to another's, nor is any man or group privileged by having more freedom to fulfill his needs. All work together to come to agreement on the goals to be sought and at least the general means to be employed. Rational persuasion based on love and esteem, not techniques of domination, would prevail, Sartre says.[7]

This means that in a direct democracy there would have

to be a complete openness of man to man. In order to maintain genuine bonds of solidarity and to work effectively for the real good of all, men would have to reveal their basic needs and desires to each other. "A man's existence must be entirely visible to his neighbor, whose own existence must be entirely visible in turn, before true social harmony can be established."[8] Men must be able to share their individual insights and approaches as to the optimum ways of directing society for the common good. A direct democracy demands that all citizens attain the knowledge that will enable them to participate effectively in self-government, since no elite group will have this function as its special privilege. This means, Sartre points out, that all men must be free to pursue knowledge in order to discover the viable possibilities for actions that will fulfill their common needs. Furthermore, they must be free to criticize any "established" body of truths about the human condition and its possibilities.[9]

Of course, once policies are agreed upon by the people their implementation may be the responsibility of a smaller number of expert technicians, but even here direct democracy plays a central role. For, Sartre says, the policies and their implementation must continually be guided by the masses. Those employed to concretize the policy must at every opportunity go to the people to make sure of their support, to ensure that they do not become isolated from the people's needs and desires by becoming too bureaucratic. Sartre comments favorably on the Chinese cultural revolutions, which he interprets as attempts to keep continually in touch with the masses.[10] It is in this connection that he asserts the need of *continual* revolution in society, a revolution against all tendencies toward static institutionalism, centralization of power, and bureaucratization—and calls himself an anarchist.[11] This relates to a point discussed in chapter 5. In an ideal direct democracy the group of free men would not be allowed to become an end in itself and so to evolve into a rigid bureaucratic institution. Direct democracy would help ensure the group remaining at the level of the pledged group, always taking the free development of all its members as its goal.

Thus, a direct democracy is seen by Sartre as removing, at least in the industrialized nations, the major obstacle to freedom today, the alienation of man by man. As we noted earlier, he believes that it is the powerlessness of the masses in relation to their socioeconomic-political system that constitutes their alienation today, not their lack of material necessities. The working masses are not free basically because they do not have control over their destiny, and this is because they do not control the substructures and superstructures of their society. Direct democracy would remedy this. Of course, scarcity remains a world-wide phenomenon, and only when it is eliminated will all men be free and able to live in harmony. Only then will the mutual openness referred to above be fully possible. But the abolition of scarcity will itself occur only if the alienated masses gain the power to control their destiny; the present ruling classes actually use scarcity to maintain their position of dominance.

Another feature of Marx's classless society that leads Sartre to identify it with his ideal free society is that in it the division of labor is abolished. Marx himself had suggested that it is this division that gives rise to different classes struggling with each other, and Sartre apparently agrees. He suggests that in the ideal society men will be both intellectual and manual workers; the two will not be divided into separate specialized classes. He likes what he has seen in some Israeli kibbutzim: " a shepherd . . . who reads, reflects, writes, in looking after his sheep."[12] One is reminded of Marx's statement that in the classless society with the division of labor abolished "it [is] possible for me to do one thing to-day and another to-morrow, to hunt in the morning, fish in the afternoon, rear cattle in the evening, criticize after dinner . . . without ever becoming hunter, fisherman, shepherd or critic."[13] True social harmony and cooperation are extremely difficult in a society of specialists having little or no understanding of the contribution made by those in different fields. Such specialization results in rivalry and competition, not common action. Furthermore, an integral development of *all* of man's capacities and a fulfillment of *all* of his needs is practically unattainable where specialization based on the division of labor is prominent.

This last point brings us to the question of the kind of culture that would be present in a classless society of free men. Sartre himself admits he often wonders about this, but offers few suggestions. In line with his stress on the sovereignty of the people, he does say that such a culture will be determined by the people themselves and will be for the benefit of all. One of his criticisms of capitalism is that in it culture is a bourgeois monopoly and the worker is, therefore, deprived of his share of the intellectual and aesthetic life.[14] The classless society will include the great works of art produced under capitalism but will make them available to all. It will preserve these masters but in a new form and context, one impossible to describe at present, he says.[15]

Though this vagueness about specifics is typical of his statements about the ideal free society, Sartre's basic identification of the classless society with his "free milieu of free individuals" is intelligible. His embrace of Marxism on this point is hardly a radical conversion from his existentialism. Sartre believes that Marxism's analysis of the causes of the alienation of freedom in contemporary society is accurate, and that its goal, true socialism, is in fact what must be attained to achieve the free society. "Socialism," he writes, "is freedom choosing itself as the goal."[16]

If we put this in terms of morality, we could say that in general that conduct which promotes freedom for all is morally good, that which impedes it is morally evil. And this is the same as saying that anything which promotes the coming of the classless society is morally good, that which impedes it is evil. Note that, as I said once before, this is clearly a teleological ethical theory in the traditional sense. What is central is the goal to be attained. Setting forth moral rules for determining the morality of specific kinds of acts or of individual acts, while important, is secondary. I mention this because I suspect that many have come away with the impression that there is no ethics in Sartre's and de Beauvoir's works because they have been looking there for a list of specific moral rules by which to guide and judge man's conduct. As a matter of fact, some such norms are suggested by them, but it is certainly true that they make little effort to enumerate them or to defend those they do mention.

I have already offered one reason for this—namely, their emphasis on the moral ideal of freedom for all in a classless society. The overall orientation of an individual's or a society's conduct and its consequences are of major moral import, the character of particular acts or classes of acts is not. It is the fundamental project, the choice of primary values, that is central. No doubt such choices will involve acts to realize these values, but these acts must be seen in their total orientation, not in isolation. Too many works on ethics deal with acts and classes of acts in abstraction, ignoring the fact that in an individual or a society of individuals there are many interrelated acts forming a whole. The moral character of this gestalt of acts can be determined only in terms of their overall orientation and direction, which indicate the primary value that is sought.[17] The same acts in one context might be highly moral because they promote freedom for all; yet in another context the exact opposite might be the case. A given act viewed in isolation might appear morally insignificant or evil, but in its general direction and its concrete unity with other acts be highly moral. To take a simple example, acts of torture would seem clearly to involve denial of the freedom of others, and Sartre has vehemently condemned them. But he has condemned them only when done by oppressors—for example, French bent on maintaining Algiers as a colony—not when done by those he believed were using torture as a last resort and as part of general strategy to attain their freedom. It is, therefore, impossible to say what the moral character of a given act or class of acts is in isolation from its unity with other acts possessing a total orientation. Sartre simply does not subscribe to the view that there are any acts or classes of acts that are always and everywhere morally good or morally evil. This is not to say that general moral judgments may not be made about classes of acts, judgments which hold for the most part. But certainly no absolutely universal statements about the morality of acts are possible.

There is, I believe, another equally important reason why Sartre and de Beauvoir have not taken pains to set forth specific moral rules to guide conduct. That is their insistence (which we have mentioned before) that individual salvation is impossible. They believe that today's milieu of oppression, violence, and alienation makes it ridiculous to expect many individuals to live lives of moral purity striving for the freedom of all men. In our day even the most well-meaning person cannot help but support structures that impede the human development of many. Furthermore, there are many whose freedom is so alienated that it would be ludicrous to expect them to respect, let alone promote, the freedom of others. The entire socioeconomic world structure must be transformed before all men can be expected to effectively promote freedom for all. Men must be liberated before a morality of freedom involving free men choosing each other's freedom can be created, Sartre says: "First all men must be able to become men by the improvement of their conditions of existence so that a universal morality can be created. . . . What matters first is the liberation of man."[18] I believe it is the absolute priority which he places on the revolutionary revision of society that best explains why Sartre has devoted a major portion of his last twenty-five years to achieving this rather than elaborating moral norms to guide individual conduct. Some have objected that this priority in no way prevented him from offering moral norms to guide conduct toward achieving the liberation of men.[19] They have pointed to the fact that he has never hesitated to take stands on particular issues—for example, the Algerian and Viet Nam wars, the student rebellion of 1968, the Portuguese revolution, the workers' seizure of the Renault factory—and have argued that if he can take such stands he can offer specific moral norms.

I am sympathetic to this objection, but it needs to be

tempered. For one thing, Sartre and de Beauvoir have offered such norms, though they have spent little time deriving, defending, or discussing them. For another, once the supreme moral principle is established it does not seem particularly difficult to supply specific moral norms geared to its attainment. In general, anything promoting freedom for all in the classless society is morally good; anything impeding it is evil. Now, more specifically, acts such as torture, killing of innocent people, lying, cowardice, betrayal, apathy, all of which frustrate or fail to support freedom, have been condemned by these existentialists. On the positive side, courage, fidelity, justice, commitment, honesty, love, and esteem have been approved[20]—all in the name of freedom for all. The real difficulties are not in supplying such specific norms but in making moral judgments in the concrete order. Is this particular strike, this rebellion, this government policy, or this way of treating women or the elderly good or bad? These are the especially tough moral questions, and I believe it is to their credit that Sartre and de Beauvoir have continually addressed themselves to them. Of course, it would have been better if they had indicated which specific moral norms are to be applied where, whether or not there is a hierarchy of such norms, and under what precise circumstances exceptions to them can be allowed. But in the face of all that they have done and written, this criticism, though valid, loses some of its force.

I conclude this section with a brief discussion of Sartre's and de Beauvoir's views of violence. It is violence against the freedom of others that appears most clearly to violate the moral norms they recognize. I mentioned earlier that Sartre has excused the use of torture and other violent terrorist tactics by those who had no other means to free themselves from oppression. At one time he seemed willing to condone even the excesses of Stalinism as unfortunately necessary for the revolution to produce the classless society.[21] More generally, both Sartre and de Beauvoir believe that in a world full of oppression and scarcity it is simply impossible to promote every man's freedom all of the time. In such a world, it is absurd to think that rigid, oppressive institutions can be changed without violence. Conflict of freedoms is inevitable; to act so as to promote some people's freedom will inevitably mean denying that of others. Obviously, if we are genuinely interested in freedom for all we cannot allow all men to do whatever they please, whatever they freely choose—for some choose to destroy or enslave others.[22] In order to promote the freedom of the greatest number, I will have to frustrate the freedom of those who are themselves out to destroy the freedom of many. The man who will not fight the oppressor becomes an accomplice of his oppression. Clearly, then, violence against an oppressor's freedom is justifiable. Add to this the fact that Sartre in particular sees a tremendous number of oppressors in our world. Anyone who, by his acceptance of the rewards of a political-economic system, implicitly supports that system is responsible to some degree for the oppression of freedom that system visits on others. It follows that violence against oppressors means violence against a great many people indeed.

Violence against oppressors of freedom, even when "oppressor" is defined broadly, is one thing; but Sartre and de Beauvoir have gone further and excused, albeit somewhat reluctantly, violence even against the innocent. They have done this when such violence seemed to be the only way of achieving freedom for the greater number. In a recent interview, in response to the assertion that he supports violence, Sartre replied: "I have always approved of the violent act by which man affirms his freedom and his solidarity with the oppressed . . . I approve of the violent act that is directed toward establishing a just and equal society."[23] Clearly, not any and all violence is justified in his eyes; yet it is equally clear that any which is directed toward establishing "a just and equal society" is. This sounds like the old dictum "the end justifies the means." That somewhat oversimplifies his position, however, for some violent acts are such that they are incompatible with the goal to be attained: "in the majority of cases . . . the means employed introduce a *qualitative* alteration into the end," Sartre once wrote.[24] Accordingly, he attacked the brutal suppression of the Hungarian freedom fighters because the Soviets defended socialism "by methods which are closely related to Tsarist repression."[25] And he is critical of any revolution that would try to achieve freedom from oppression by lying to and thus oppressing men.

> May one perpetuate oppression with the pretext of putting an end to it? Is it necessary to enslave man in order the better to free him? It will be said that the means is transitory. Not if it helps create a *lied-to* and *lying* mankind; for then . . . the reasons one had for abolishing oppression are undermined by the way he goes about abolishing it.[26]

What particularly strikes me in the above text is the clear implication that, if the means of oppression were transitory and did serve to abolish, not perpetuate, oppression in the long run, they would be justified in Sartre's eyes. I believe that, in fact, this is his position; and it explains how he has been able to support the terrorism of the Viet Cong, the FLN, the Palestinians, and the Baader-Meinhoff gang, and to call for an all-out Soviet nuclear strike against the U.S., even though such actions would kill admittedly innocent people.[27]

Actually, de Beauvoir has addressed herself to this issue much more thoroughly than has Sartre. She devotes much of *The Ethics* to grappling with the problem of justifying violence against innocent people.[28] She shows herself to be very sensitive to the dangers of legitimizing such violence in the name of utility. Yet, in the final analysis, she reluctantly admits that it is legitimate, provided of course that it is truly useful and necessary for the overall liberation of men. She concludes, "it is therefore logical, though this logic implies an outrageous absurdity to prefer the salvation of the greater number,"[29] and thus to sacrifice the lesser. This involves an "outrageous absurdity" because it sacrifices freedom to promote freedom. Such a sacrifice is justifiable, de Beauvoir indicates, as a last resort after all other alternatives have been exhausted, when it is clearly necessary in the concrete situation to prevent even greater evils and attain specific goals that genuinely promote freedom. Furthermore, it is justifiable only when it has a good chance of preventing greater evils or attaining specific goods, which prevention or attainment is extremely significant in promoting the overall liberation of men, and only when it is temporary and will not establish permanently repressive structures.

This willingness to condone violence within limits seems reasonable to me. In some situations men simply do not have the luxury of a choice between good and evil, but only among various evils. In such cases, to choose the lesser of these evils is itself the best choice. Sartre's, and especially de Beauvoir's, analysis of the conditions under which violence even against innocents is admissible makes sense, as does their view that to refrain from any and all violence results in becoming the accomplice of the violence of others. I suspect that what scandalizes some is not the philosophical views of these existentialists on this issue but their support of the violence of specific groups. I would not claim that I can understand how they have justified all the violence they have supported, even in terms of their own principles. However, I leave the investigation of this to others with more knowledge of the political scene in Europe, and in France in particular.

Though violence on occasion is justifiable and exceptions to general moral norms are always possible, there is, of course, no exception to the obligation to promote the freedom of all men, or at least "the salvation of the greater number." (Incidentally, to speak of the salvation of the greater number should not be taken in simply a quantitative sense. Both existentialists explicitly say that qualitative factors must also be included.)[30] Since there is no exception to the primary obligation to promote freedom, it is possible, as we have said, to come to general, not universally absolute, conclusions concerning the morality of certain conduct. Of course, norms like those given above, though more specific than the simple exhortation to act for the freedom of the greatest number, are still quite general, and their particular application in concrete situations remains unclear. It is also unclear whether such norms (lying, torture, and murder are wrong; justice, honesty, and respect are good) are hierarchically arranged and under what conditions exceptions are allowed. No doubt more explanation of ethical rules and more guidance as to their application can be offered than these existentialists do. There is the danger of going too far in this direction, however. The danger is that of casuistry, of forgetting that moral decisions are ultimately the prudential judgment of the situated, free individual. After all, as de Beauvoir says, "Ethics does not furnish recipes."[31]

B. CRITICAL EVALUATION

Perhaps a word about the apparent popular influence of Sartrean ethics in our day would be an appropriate beginning to this final section. Many systems of ethics have included freedom as one of the values that they uphold. However, to make freedom the *primary* value in morality, as Sartre and de Beauvoir do, and to consider everything else as morally good only insofar as it promotes freedom are highly unusual. Yet it is this combination that makes Sartrean ethics so topical. Who would deny that freedom is taken by many today as a crucially important value, and by some as the absolutely primary value? From the emerging nations of the Third World to the ghettos of our large cities, thousands have been willing to risk everything for freedom. In recent years higher education in America has seen significant changes in college and university curricula in the name of freedom. The minimizing or even abolition of traditional course and credit-hour requirements has taken place in many cases, not because educators believed that students would thereby achieve greater knowledge or a better education but because they viewed such requirements as inimical to the freedom of their students. Freedom became more important than education, with very questionable results. The ongoing abortion controversy provides another illustration. Proponents of abortion on demand frequently cite freedom of choice to support their position. For them the value of this freedom takes primacy over the value of life itself. More generally, men's reaction against "the system"—against the anonymous, computerized bureaucracy threatening to turn them into automatons—testifies to the value they place on their individual freedom. The phrase "do your own thing" is simply one popular expression of this value. I cannot help but believe that Sartrean ethical thought, which champions freedom as man's highest value, has been a significant influence on this moral and intellectual climate.

Hazel Barnes has written that Sartre's own life and works offer visible proof that an ethics of good faith is possible.[32] Though I do not accept this statement entirely, I certainly share the feeling behind it. Whether one agrees with the particular stances he has taken in the political arena or not, Sartre's sense of responsibility and his commitment to the wretched of the earth deserve admiration. His unceasing efforts as an intellectual on behalf of the oppressed, his unwillingness to settle for minimal reforms when radical transformation is needed, and his impatience with those who tolerate the continuation of injustice make him the gadfly of all whose own comfort tends to desensitize them to the misery of the majority of mankind. Sartre has been accused of accentuating the negative in his portrayal of our world. Perhaps that is so. But may this not be exactly what the comfortable need to hear, lest we consider our condition to be the universal human lot? It is too easy for us, particularly if we are intellectuals, to fail to hear the voice of the oppressed. We need a fellow petit bourgeois intellectual to shout it at us. As long as Sartre lives, it is just a little more difficult to be blind to the glaring disparities in the lives of our fellow inhabitants of this globe and to ignore our collective responsibility for this state of affairs.

Still, none of these words of praise can take the place of a careful critical analysis of the foundations and structure of Sartrean ethics. One of my main goals in writing this book was to show that the status of that ethics is not nearly as bleak as some critics have portrayed it. As a regular teacher of ethics who has perused countless surveys and anthologies for possible course use, I am continually surprised at how few authors are aware that a defensible and defended Sartrean moral theory exists. In many quarters, it is apparently a well-kept secret that Sartre and de Beauvoir have proposed and reasoned out the general outline of an ethics, that they have persuasively argued for their positions, and that what they have offered is not hopelessly vague or confused nor merely an irrational appeal to emotion. In my opinion their morality does generally hang together in its basic principles and structure, resting, of course, on Sartre's ontology. More specifically, as I have stated above, I believe that within this ontology (once certain initial choices are made) their two central arguments—that which proposes freedom as the primary value, and that (de Beauvoir's) which maintains this should be the freedom of all men—are well reasoned and plausible. This is not to say that I find no difficulties in this ethics or in its reasoning; I have made it amply clear in each chapter that I do see problems. But I particularly wish to stress here, since few English-speaking philosophers appear cognizant of it, that a credible and coherent Sartrean moral theory, at least in general structure, has been presented by these philosophers.

Furthermore, as we have seen, theirs is not a morality that advocates total relativism or license, for it proposes a common value for all men to follow—freedom. It is not solipsistic, anarchistic, nor totally individualistic, for it calls upon each man to promote the freedom of all. Nor is this value itself completely vacuous, for it is specified by man's basic needs and their fulfillment. It is, perhaps, a severe and difficult ethics, for it demands that man accept responsibility for being the only creator of meaning in a sterile universe. Yet it is not nihilistic, for it does not claim that human existence must forever remain without value; nor pessimistic, since it says that life will be as meaningful as man himself makes it.

I believe it has also been shown that this ethical theory

does not involve wholesale rejection of the ontology of *Being and Nothingness,* as critics such as Mary Warnock have claimed. We have seen that Sartre's subjectivism in value, far from rendering ethics impossible, supplies the very basis of his (and de Beauvoir's) claim that freedom should be man's primary value, and their insistence that man can create a meaningful existence for himself. Similarly, their belief that man is a failure insofar as he necessarily desires to be God becomes in their eyes the impetus for him to undergo a radical conversion and seek salvation in the human realm alone, especially by entering into positive relations with other free subjects from whom he can obtain value and meaning. Speaking of human relations, while it is true that Sartre has moved to a more balanced and positive view of them since he wrote *Being and Nothingness,* I have argued that even in that early work he did not forever bar the possibility of relationships of harmony and friendship. In this connection, his movement from the ethics promised in 1943 to an emphasis on social-political philosophy is intelligible, not because he categorically repudiated the ontology he held in the forties, but because he has rejected an individual ethics of personal salvation and come to believe that a radical transformation of society is necessary before men can live fully authentic lives.

It is interesting to note, as I have on occasion, that in some respects Sartrean ethics is quite traditional. Like Aristotelianism, hedonism, utilitarianism, ethics of self-fulfillment, and others, it is teleological in character, for it judges the morality of men and actions in terms of a goal. It also proposes an ideal common to the entire Western humanistic moral tradition, the fulfillment of man's basic needs and potentialities. Furthermore, when we refer to its ideal, as we did in the last section, as the greatest freedom for the greatest number, this clearly suggests affinities with traditional utilitarian theory—with freedom, of course, taking the place of happiness (or pleasure) as the primary goal. I would not want to exaggerate this similarity, however, for as far as the *foundations* of the respective ethics are concerned, the differences are pronounced. Thus, the primary exponent of utilitarianism, John Stuart Mill, argues that the general happiness should be man's basic value because that is the goal men seek above all else.[33] But neither Sartre nor de Beauvoir has proposed such an argument as regards freedom. They never say that men should take the freedom of all as their fundamental moral value because that is the goal they basically seek above all others. In fact, they do not believe that man desires freedom as his primary end; rather, they believe he wants to be God. And they do not advise him to choose to value this goal because he desires it. Quite the contrary. Mill and other utilitarians, as well as teleologists in general, are often prime examples of ethicians who are charged with committing the naturalistic fallacy, holding that because something is desired it must, therefore, be chosen as a value. As I explained at length in chapter 3, Sartrean ethics does not succumb to this charge, and to that degree it is quite different from many of these traditional theories.

Having said all this in support of Sartre's and de Beauvoir's moral theory, I remain convinced that serious problems, many of which I have discussed earlier, are present in it. Though the ethics overall is coherent and generally hangs together, it is certainly not logically airtight. My quarrel is not with the pragmatic value of many of the positions Sartre takes. His stress on individual freedom and responsibility and on man's ability collectively to control his destiny is most welcome in a world becoming increasingly dominated by faceless bureaucracies. One wonders what changes would take place if men could be convinced that they are not totally passive and powerless in relation to "the system" but that they in fact produce the system and so can change it. I agree with Sartre that such a realization is necessary if an era of true humanism is to arise on a large scale. I am sympathetic, too, with his recent emphasis on direct democracy. If we believe that man is free by nature and in his choices and if we value this freedom, then we must take seriously Sartre's suggestion that this should be translated politically into the sovereignty of *all* men over their social and political institutions, which sovereignty demands something like direct democracy. I confess to some doubt as to whether it can work on a large scale; I have seen it work at New England town meetings. In any case, there is plenty of room in our present political structures for more movement in that direction, toward debureaucratization, decentralization, and democratization. However, there remains something that needs to be challenged even in Sartre's insistence on direct democracy.

I am bothered by what seems to be his almost blind faith in the moral judgment of the oppressed. We have pointed out that Sartre now sees his function as an intellectual to serve as the mouthpiece of the masses. I do not fault his decision to serve the underprivileged. But at the basis of this decision is his belief that the masses are striving for a truly universal equalitarian society and so are inevitably moral in their efforts to alleviate their condition; that they "demand liberty for themselves and for everyone"; that the workers when they revolt "are completely moral because they are not exploiting anyone."[34] This strikes me as incredibly naïve. For one thing, the masses themselves are hardly a monolithic group but rather a conglomeration of groups, institutions, and serial individuals. There are plenty of differences among these various segments. All this is admitted by Sartre. Yet, as far as I can see, he offers no way to determine which segment is pursuing morally good values, which segment at least implicitly has the classless society as its goal. Furthermore, I question whether there is evidence to support the idea that the oppressed are in general less selfish, less prone to oppression, more committed to the freedom and well-being of all men than the bourgeoisie. Pettiness, inhumanity, and callous disregard of the welfare of others are hardly the privileged possessions of the latter, as Sartre at times seems to suggest. Even when he admits the presence of these faults in the masses he offers no criterion by which one might distinguish their true needs, aspirations, and values from false ones. I referred to this in chapter 3. Though he verbally distinguishes between real and artificial human needs, nowhere does he propose any basis for this distinction or any reason why men should fulfill the former and not the latter. I do not reject the value of close cooperation between intellectuals and workers, nor underestimate the danger of pontificating intellectuals who are out of touch with humanity. If one believes in the freedom of all men and values this freedom, it follows that all men must have input, significantly more input than they have at present, in determining the values that form their society and hence their lives. But this is far from making the masses the last word when it comes to judgments of morality. It is true that the Russian brand of Marxist socialism no longer has the privileged position for Sartre that it once did. Its place has been taken by the nebulous entity called the masses.

His references to the masses, as if they are a single unified group pursuing common values that are *ipso facto* moral, strike me as especially incongruous in the light of what I have called the Hobbesian character of Sartre's thought about human society. As I discussed at length in chapters 4 and 5, he has never, except perhaps very recently, ceased to view men as ruggedly individualistic. In his eyes they do not naturally tend to join together and cooperate in love and friendship for any lasting period of time; rather, they can only be held together by force of fear. Sartre adopts this Hobbesian perspective, as I have pointed out, because he believes that each man desires to be God, the sole cause of his own being, and thus is naturally protective of his personal freedom and suspicious of any influence on it by others. If he has, indeed, changed his position on this, I welcome it, but it would be a change for which he has offered no explanation. As far as his belief that man desires to be a *causa sui* is concerned, I seriously questioned it in chapter 2, and I see no need to repeat that criticism here. I will simply say again that I find little evidence that all men are concerned about preserving their individual freedom in relation to others, or that they fundamentally desire to be the sole cause of the meaning of their existence. In any case Sartre's conception of man's fundamental desire has from the beginning seriously biased his understanding of human relations. It has caused him to constantly accentuate the negative, the difficulties, the problems of human unity, and to downgrade the positive. If he does now have, as some recent interviews seem to show, a more positive and balanced view of man's social dimension, one can only remark that it has taken him a long time to recognize what most human beings know from childhood, that love and trust among men are realities that are at least as prominent in human experience as disharmony, suspicion, and conflict.

In the remainder of this chapter I focus my attention on the central arguments offered by these existentialists to establish their basic ethical positions. Some of what I say repeats earlier criticisms. I have already said that I believe their reasoning is intelligible and plausible but not totally valid. In chapter 3 I presented their basic argument for the choice of freedom as primary value—namely, that man should choose to value freedom above all else since it is the source of all meaning and value, including any value his existence has. One of the problems with this argument, as I have already pointed out, is the ambiguity present in Sartre's and de Beauvoir's explanations of what it means to value freedom, an ambiguity that arises because they are inconsistent in their use of the term "value." Thus, to value freedom means in one case to accept the fact that man is free by nature and should not pretend otherwise. In another case it means to attempt to *increase* freedom of choice and the fulfillment of human needs. As far as the argument itself is concerned, what it demonstrates is that man should value his free choice and the structure that is its foundation. It does not show that man should necessarily strive to increase this free choice by increasing attainable goals. (For this criticism in more detail, see chapter 3, section D.)

There are further difficulties. Their argument maintains that the choice of freedom as supreme value is the *most consistent* choice in view of the ontological fact that freedom alone creates all meaning and values. (Sartre explicitly emphasizes this note of consistency.) If I am to truly value any values I create, including the meaning I give my life, I must value the freedom from which they come. The choice of freedom as a value is logically entailed in the choice of any other value. Now, I think this argument is sound but, as I noted in chapter 3, to accept it demands prior choice—namely, the choice to value a meaningful or justified life, as well as the choice to value logic and consistency. And these choices, Sartre and de Beauvoir admit, are arbitrary. Neither a meaningful existence, nor logical consistency, nor consistency with reality has any intrinsic value, nor can *compelling* reasons be given for valuing any one of them. However, this is not what particularly bothers me here. To admit that no logically compelling reasons can be given for valuing a meaningful life is not to advance a fatal criticism of Sartrean ethics. If it is, I suspect all ethical theories would be vulnerable, since their ultimate principles, precisely because they are ultimate, are always beyond logical proof, strictly speaking. My present concern is that, even if man does value the attaining of a meaningful existence, this does not require him to value logic or consistency with reality. A meaningful existence—that is, one that has value—can be achieved by valuing irrationality, or nonrationality, or even escape from reality. If a person chooses to value a life of radically inconsistent behavior with no intelligible plan or purpose, or a life based on feelings ("whatever turns you on!"), or a life of escape from reality (for example, via drugs), such a life will have value and meaning by his very choice of it. If he can convince others to value it also, it will have even more meaning. To be sure, it would be the individual's freedom that creates such values; and it would be more consistent, therefore, for him to value this freedom. It would be illogical for him to value the goals freedom chooses and yet not to value freedom itself. However, consistency and logic would be meaningful only to one who has chosen to value consistency with facts and logical implication. And there is no compelling reason to so choose. Either Sartre and de Beauvoir have in spite of themselves presumed logic and consistency to be of intrinsic value; or, more likely, they believe there is a necessary entailment between the choice of a meaningful life, a life having value, and the choice of logic and consistency with reality. Unfortunately, they do not argue for this entailment, nor do I see any necessary connection.

An equally bothersome feature of the argument for freedom as the supreme value is that it seems in fact to propose the primacy of a meaningful, valuable existence, rather than the primacy of freedom. Freedom is valued as the most consistent and logical means to attaining a meaningful life. If I am correct on this, and if I am also right in saying that valuing a meaningful existence does not necessarily mean valuing logical consistency or consistency with reality, it is even clearer that singling out freedom is somewhat arbitrary.

A similar criticism can be made of the argument de Beauvoir offers to show that each man should value the freedom of all men. I mentioned earlier that though I think it is a good argument it does not in fact demonstrate that the freedom of *all* men should be valued. Furthermore, to the extent it works, it works only if, again, one gives prior value to a meaningful existence. Recall that the argument rests on the fact that other human beings are the only place, outside of myself, from which to obtain value for my existence. Now, suppose others, even my peers, do value my life, do declare it to be meaningful. Is this enough to make it so, especially if I am not promoting the freedom of all? Was Hitler's life a morally valuable one because millions acclaimed him? Obviously, Sartre and de Beauvoir do not think so, for Hitler did not seek freedom for all. But, then, if freedom is in fact the primary value, as long as a man's acts truly do promote it, his life is one of moral value. It matters little how others evaluate him. If they do not approve of his efforts in behalf of freedom, they are wrong (either because of ignorance or bad faith), not he. The life of a Solzhenitsyn would be no less valuable if he won the approval of no one. Clearly, the problem with making a meaningful existence, a life having value, the primary goal is that it does not follow from this that freedom, either my own or anyone else's, need be valued. There are many ways to obtain the free approval of one's free peers: the way of Hitler and Stalin, no less than that of Gandhi and Martin Luther King, Jr. It is true that de Beauvoir insists that man does not seek just anyone's positive valuation, but his peers'. Perhaps she would claim that one's peers could only be those who take freedom as their ultimate value, that approval from men with other primary values is not what man seeks. However, she does not actually say this nor argue for it, and in fact it seems contrary to human experience.

The primacy these philosophers place on the value of a meaningful existence raises perhaps the most central question of all. At the beginning of this book I stated that Sartrean moral philosophy is an attempt to live in the face of the death of God and the absence of all objective values. It attempts to say how man can live meaningfully in an intrinsically meaningless universe. Does it succeed? In one sense the answer must surely be yes. Since the very word "meaningful" has sense only in relation to man, since there is no transcendent realm of meaning, there can be success on the human scale. Men through their choices can and do give human existence meaning and value. That man-given meaning cannot totally satisfy a creature who, according to Sartre, desires to be God is true; man forever remains, he says, "an unhappy consciousness with no possibility of surpassing its unhappy state."[35] Still, this is the best man can attain in a universe where he alone is the origin of all values. Man is encouraged to attain a meaningful existence by living authentically, by choosing freedom for all men. But this is precisely the problem. Is there ultimately any good reason why he should identify a life of meaning and value with an authentic life?

On the very last pages of her *Ethics*, de Beauvoir writes that since man creates all values,

> all glorification of the earth is true as soon as it is realized. Let men attach value to words, forms, colors, mathematical theorems, physical laws, and athletic prowess; let them accord value to one another in love

and friendship, and the objects, the events, and the men immediately *have* this value; they have it absolutely.[36]

Yet, it is equally true that in a Sartrean universe ugliness, ignorance, murder, rape, and slavery *have* value if man chooses them to. Why should he choose to value what de Beauvoir lists rather than the opposite? Again, why should he choose to live authentically and promote the freedom of all? Sartre's and de Beauvoir's answers rest on the arguments they offer for the choice of freedom for all, arguments I have already analyzed and found plausible but inadequate. I cannot see how they can be made more decisive, short of conceding some intrinsic and objective value to logic, consistency with reality, and a meaningful human existence, as well as to all human freedom. Yet such a concession would seriously undermine Sartre's ontology.

Of course, whether he chooses to value freedom or not, whether he chooses to live authentically or not, man can create a meaningful existence for himself and others. Man can create values in a universe that in itself has none. To be sure, its intrinsic sterility remains. And Sartre, unlike Camus in *The Myth of Sisyphus*, does not pretend that man can ultimately be happy as a Sisyphus engaged in intrinsically meaningless tasks. Man remains a useless passion, an unhappy consciousness. Even the advent of the classless society, the free milieu of free individuals, cannot satisfy his deepest desire—to attain a self-given necessity for his being.[37] In a most revealing interview about ten years ago Sartre was asked, "What are we saved by?" He replied, "By nothing. There is no salvation anywhere. The idea of salvation implies the idea of an absolute . . . . The absolute is gone. There remain countless tasks." He was then asked if he still saw the universe, as he did in *Nausea*, as fundamentally absurd. His response was affirmative:

> the universe remains dark. We are animals struck by catastrophe . . . . But I discovered suddenly that alienation, exploitation of man by man, undernourishment, relegated to the background metaphysical evil which is

a luxury. Hunger is an evil: period. A Soviet citizen, an official writer, once said to me: "The day when Communism (that is, well-being for everyone) reigns, man's tragedy will begin: his finitude." It is not yet time to reveal it.[38]

The problem is that Sartre has already revealed it. While it may be truly heroic to devote oneself to countless tasks to attain "well-being for everyone," knowing that salvation is impossible, the fact is that these tasks to attain well-being for all have no intrinsic significance, nor does well-being itself. I can admit that Sisyphus is heroic; I find it impossible to imagine him happy. Of course, happiness has no intrinsic value anyway in Sartre's universe—but then neither does heroism!

I earlier voiced my suspicion that Sartre and de Beauvoir have in spite of themselves accepted the existence of intrinsic values—namely, those of logical consistency and consistency with reality. I would like to return to this point in my closing remarks, for their very lives seem to call into question their claim that all values are ultimately subjective and due to individual freedom. Since their days in the French resistance movement, neither of them has lived and worked as if the freedom of their fellow-men and a meaningful human existence consistent with reality are values arbitrarily created by their personal free choices—values, then, just as easily uncreated. Their willingness to put their lives and honor on the line in support of human dignity seems to bear witness to the very spirit of seriousness they so scornfully reject. I suppose this should not be surprising, since men seem to be naturally serious. Cross-cultural studies have shown the presence in all human societies of a number of commonly accepted general values.[39] To claim that this is mere coincidence, that men in radically different cultures and societies just happened to create the same values, seems preposterous. Far more likely is it that this widespread agreement is rooted in man's discovery that certain acts, relationships, and ways of doing things possess objective value for the kind of being he is, a being with specific needs and desires. If "Hunger is an evil: period," might not nourishment (or knowledge, love, justice, etc.) be a good: period?

Notes

CHAPTER 1

1. This information on Sartre's ethical writings is found in the invaluable work by M. Contat and M. Rybalka, *The Writings of Jean-Paul Sartre, A Bibliographical Life*, vol. 1, trans. Richard McCleary (Evanston: Northwestern University Press, 1974). See their index entry entitled "Ethics, morality." Sartre's near blindness was acknowledged by him in a recent interview, "Self-Portrait at Seventy," in *Life/Situations*, trans. P. Auster and L. Davis (New York: Pantheon Books, 1977), pp. 3–6.

2. Simone de Beauvoir, *Force of Circumstance*, trans. Richard Howard (New York: G. P. Putnam's Sons, 1964), p. 67.

3. "The Purpose of Writing," an interview published in Sartre's *Between Existentialism and Marxism*, trans. John Matthews (London: NLB, 1974), p. 10. He had said the same thing in an article fourteen years earlier whose title clearly makes the point—"We Write for Our Own Time," trans. Sylvia Glass, *Virginia Quarterly Review* 23 (April 1947).

4. Interview with John Gerassi in *New York Times Magazine*, October 17, 1971, entitled "Sartre Accuses the Intellectuals of Bad Faith." The entire work, *On a raison de se révolter*, Ph. Gavi, J.-P. Sartre, P. Victor (Paris: Gallimard, 1974), a collection of interviews which took place after 1968, makes

frequent references to the impact on him of those turbulent days of May.

5. "Self-Portrait at Seventy," p. 53. See also *On a raison de se révolter*, pp. 40, 248.

6. Gerassi interview, p. 38. "A Friend of the People," an interview published in Sartre's *Between Existentialism and Marxism*, p. 296, expresses this position, as does Francis Jeanson, *Sartre dans sa vie* (Paris: Éditions du Seuil, 1974), p. 267.

7. *Sartre dans sa vie*, p. 267.

8. *On a raison de se révolter*, pp. 45, 53, 76, 118. See also *Sartre dans sa vie*, pp. 266–268.

9. "Self-Portrait at Seventy," pp. 60, 74.

10. In *Sartre dans sa vie*, pp. 266–268, Jeanson designates Sartre's idealism as his ignoring of the social dimension of the individual. In "Materialism and Revolution," *Literary and Philosophical Essays*, trans. Annette Michelson (New York: Collier Books, 1962), Sartre refers to idealism as the view that some men have intrinsic rights, p. 236.

11. "A Long, Bitter, Sweet Madness," interview with *Le Monde*, trans. Anthony Hartley and published in *Encounter* 22, no. 6 (June 1964): 61; "The Purpose of Writing," p. 27; *The Words*, trans. B. Frechtman (Greenwich, Conn.: Fawcett Publications, Inc., 1966), pp. 157–160.

12. Unpublished notes of Sartre's quoted by de Beauvoir in *Force of Circumstance*, p. 199.

13. *The Writings of Jean-Paul Sartre*, pp. 249–252; "A Long, Bitter, Sweet Madness," 62. This is why in *Saint Genet: Actor and Martyr*, trans. B. Frechtman (New York: New American Library, Mentor Books, 1963), a work published during this period, he referred to morality as impossible, yet inevitable (pp. 207, 247). Morality is inevitable because men must and will choose moral values for which to live; it is impossible because in our world one cannot perform acts of moral purity.

14. C. A. Van Peursen, "In gesprek met Jean-Paul Sartre," *Wending* (The Hague) 9 (March 1954): 18–20, 22–24. It is worth mentioning that de Beauvoir's *The Ethics of Ambiguity*, trans. B. Frechtman (New York: Philosophical Library, 1948), written during this period (1947), was later sharply criticized by her as too "abstract," pp. 67–68 of *Force of Circumstance*.

15. "A Plea for Intellectuals," a lecture of Sartre's published in *Between Existentialism and Marxism*, p. 259. A similar point is made in "A Long, Bitter, Sweet Madness," 62.
16. *The Writings of Jean-Paul Sartre*, p. 449. A few pages of it were published as "Determinism and Freedom," in vol. 2 of that work.
17. See pp. 70–77 and 104–106 in *On a raison de se révolter*, for example. See also "What's Jean-Paul Sartre Thinking Lately?", an interview by P. Bénichou in *Esquire* 78 (December 1972): 286.
18. "Self-Portrait at Seventy," pp. 74–76. But in these same pages he mentions that there is a remote possibility that he will return to this work again, and he indicates that in its present state it is "unfinished and obscure."
19. Hazel Barnes, *Sartre* (New York: J. B. Lippincott Co., 1973); Wilfrid Desan, *The Tragic Finale*, rev. ed. (New York: Harper Torchbooks, 1960); Marjorie Grene, *Sartre* (New York: New Viewpoints, 1973); Mary Warnock, *The Philosophy of Sartre* (New York: Barnes and Noble, Inc., 1967). Special mention should be made of Klaus Hartmann's excellent work *Sartre's Ontology* (Evanston: Northwestern University Press, 1966), by far the most scholarly book-length study of this ontology in English.

CHAPTER 2

1. *Being and Nothingness*, trans. Hazel Barnes (New York: Philosophical Library, 1956), p. 615.
2. Ibid., p. 627.
3. Richard J. Bernstein, *Praxis and Action* (Philadelphia: University of Pennsylvania Press, 1971), p. 149; see also pp. 142, 148–152. Régis Jolivet, *Sartre: The Theology of the Absurd*, trans. W. Piersol (New York: Newman Press, 1967), pp. 30, 31, 68, had a similar complaint.
4. *Being and Nothingness*, p. 81. This analysis of Sartre's concept of God is based on pp. 80–81, 89–91.
5. *The Words*, p. 61.
6. *Being and Nothingness*, pt. 2, chap. 1, sec. 3, especially pp. 84–90; also pp. 564–567.
7. *The Transcendence of the Ego*, trans. F. Williams and R.

Kirkpatrick (New York: Noonday Press, Inc., 1957), pp. 38–42, 96–99.

8. *Being and Nothingness*, p. 38, also p. 94.
9. *Existentialism and Humanism*, trans., with an introduction, P. Mairet (London: Eyre Methuen Ltd., 1973), p. 52. *Being and Nothingness*, pp. 580 and 626.
10. Henry Veatch, *For an Ontology of Morals* (Evanston: Northwestern University Press, 1971), pp. 74–77; M. Warnock, *Existentialist Ethics* (London: Macmillan, 1967), pp. 43, 47–48; Bernstein, *Praxis and Action*, pp. 151–154; A. Plantinga, "An Existentialist's Ethics," *Review of Metaphysics* 12 (December 1958): 248–249; John Wild, "Authentic Existence: A New Approach to 'Value Theory,'" in *An Invitation to Phenomenology*, ed. J. Edie (Chicago: Quadrangle Books, 1965), pp. 62–63. A similar criticism is voiced by William Frankena, *Ethics*, 2d ed. (Englewood Cliffs, N.J.: Prentice-Hall, 1973), p. 23.
11. *Existentialist Ethics*, p. 47.
12. *Praxis and Action*, p. 152.
13. *Existentialism and Humanism*, pp. 33, 34.
14. *Being and Nothingness*, pt. 2, chap. 1, sec. 3, especially pp. 92–95; also p. 38. Some other places where Sartre discusses the notion of value are: "Consciousness of Self and Knowledge of Self," trans. Mary Ellen and N. Lawrence, in *Readings in Existential Phenomenology*, ed. N. Lawrence and D. O'Connor (Englewood Cliffs, N.J.: Prentice-Hall, Inc., 1967), p. 129; "Determinism and Freedom," p. 241; *What Is Literature?*, trans. B. Frechtman (New York: Washington Square Press, Inc., 1966), pp. 30, 37, 38. Frederick Olafson, *Principles and Persons* (Baltimore: Johns Hopkins University Press, 1967), has an interesting discussion from an analytical point of view of the subjectivity of value in Sartre, chap. 6.
15. *Being and Nothingness*, pp. 481–489, 563–570.
16. Ibid., pt. 1, chap. 1, sec. 2, pp. 23–29; pt. 4, chap. 1, sec. 1, pp. 433–441. My article "Neglected Sartrean Arguments for the Freedom of Consciousness," *Philosophy Today* 17 (Spring 1973), might be helpful on this point.
17. *Being and Nothingness*, pp. 94, 564–567.
18. Ibid., p. 626.
19. Ibid., p. 627.
20. Ibid., p. 626.

21. Ibid., p. 627.
22. Many of these suggestions are put forth in a series of rhetorical questions. Because of this, some commentators, for example Arthur Danto, *Jean-Paul Sartre* (New York: The Viking Press, 1975), p. 155, have difficulty determining just what Sartre's view is here. I believe that what Sartre is saying becomes clear once it is noted that subsequent questions in effect answer earlier ones. My interpretation of these pages of *Being and Nothingness* is the same as Jeanson's in *Le problème moral et la pensée de Sartre* (Paris: Éditions du Seuil, 1965), pp. 271–273.
23. *Being and Nothingness*, p. 599.
24. Ibid., p. 566. A similar point is made on pp. 93 and 94.
25. Ibid., p. 566.
26. Ibid., pp. 566–567.
27. Ibid., pp. 93–95.
28. Ibid., p. 95.
29. Ibid., pp. 38–39.
30. Ibid., p. 94. De Beauvoir has a similar argument, *The Ethics of Ambiguity*, pp. 14–15.
31. *Being and Nothingness*, p. 581.
32. *Situations*, vol. 4 (Paris: Gallimard, 1964), p. 196. See also "On *The Idiot of the Family*," an interview with M. Contat and M. Rybalka published in *Life/Situations*, p. 122, and *The Writings of Jean-Paul Sartre*, p. 84. Jeanson, "Les caractères existentialistes de la conduite humaine selon Jean-Paul Sartre," in *Morale Chrétienne et Requêtes Contemporaines*, by F.-M. Braun et al. (Paris: Casterman, 1954), p. 176, also says this about *Being and Nothingness*. De Beauvoir makes a similar suggestion in *The Ethics of Ambiguity*, pp. 11, 46.
33. *Existentialism and Humanism*, p. 54.
34. *The Ethics of Ambiguity*, p. 15.
35. *Being and Nothingness*, p. 93.
36. Sartre's belief that values are nonreal and that choices of values are choices to make real appears quite similar to the position of contemporary analysts such as R. M. Hare. He claims that moral statements and terms are in all cases prescriptive in character. Thus, to say x is good (valuable) is always to say x should be done, or, do x. Furthermore, the acceptance of the statement x is good consists in doing x in

the appropriate situation (similar to Sartre's view that choosing x is choosing to act so as to make it real or more real). The objection I have made to Sartre is similar to that made by G. J. Warnock and Philippa Foot to Hare, namely, that he (Hare) has singled out one of the many meanings contained in moral language and absolutized it. For a general discussion of this controversy, see W. D. Hudson, *Modern Moral Philosophy* (Garden City: Doubleday, 1970), and G. J. Warnock, *Contemporary Moral Philosophy* (New York: St. Martin's, 1967).

37. For Scheler's views, see his *Formalism in Ethics and Non-Formal Ethics of Values*, trans. Manfred Frings and Roger Funk (Evanston, Ill.: Northwestern University Press, 1973), pt. 2, chap. 1, sec. 1. Sartre's reference to Scheler occurs on page 93.
38. *Being and Nothingness*, p. 93.
39. Viktor Frankl's logotherapy is rooted in the premise that man's desire for meaning is his most fundamental need. For detail consult his books, *Man's Search for Meaning* (New York: Simon & Schuster, Inc., 1963) and *The Doctor and The Soul* (New York: Random House, Inc., 1963).
40. *Being and Nothingness*, pp. 85–90.
41. Friedrich Nietzsche, *Thus Spoke Zarathustra*, trans., with an introduction, R. J. Hollingdale (New York: Penguin Books, 1969), p. 110.

CHAPTER 3

1. *Being and Nothingness*, pp. 38–39, 95, 626.
2. Ibid., p. 581. "Consciousness of Self and Knowledge of Self," p. 142. Jeanson, *Le problème moral et la pensée de Sartre*, interprets *Being and Nothingness* as an attempt to induce man to make this purifying reflection, pp. 31, 224–226, 239–243, 270–273.
3. *Being and Nothingness*, p. 625.
4. Ibid., p. 626; see also pp. 38–39, 95. "Determinism and Freedom," p. 242; *On a raison de se révolter*, pp. 45, 78–79, 118.
5. *Being and Nothingness*, p. 626.
6. "Conversation with Jean-Paul Sartre," interview in *Oui* 4 (June 1975): 70.

7. *Existentialism and Humanism*, p. 51.
8. *What Is Literature?*, pp. 108, 192; "Materialism and Revolution," pp. 245, 253; *Critique of Dialectical Reason*, trans. Alan Sheridan-Smith (Atlantic Highlands: Humanities Press, 1976), p. 673.
9. *The Ethics of Ambiguity*, p. 24.
10. *Anti-Semite and Jew*, trans. G. Becker (New York: Schocken Books, 1948), p. 90.
11. Ibid., p. 137.
12. Ibid., p. 108.
13. Ibid., pp. 149–150.
14. *Existentialism and Humanism*, pp. 51–52.
15. Some who do this are Marjorie Grene, "Authenticity: An Existential Virtue," *Ethics* 62 (1951–1952): 270; Anthony Manser, *Sartre: A Philosophic Study* (New York: Oxford University Press, 1966), p. 157; Robert Olson, "Authenticity, Metaphysics, and Moral Responsibility," *Philosophy* 34 (1959): 106–107.
16. *Existentialism and Humanism*, p. 51.
17. *Being and Nothingness*, p. 627.
18. *The Ethics of Ambiguity*, p. 24; pp. 24–26 contain her argument.
19. Ibid., p. 24. On the identification of being moral and being justified, see pp. 41, 72.
20. Ibid., p. 14.
21. Danto, *Jean-Paul Sartre*, pp. 155–157, and Manser, *Sartre*, chaps. 9 and 10, show no awareness of the argument. Olafson, *Principles and Persons*, p. 203, admits that Sartre offers a "sketch of such an argument" but seems unaware that de Beauvoir fills in the sketch. Actually, Olafson's own proposal for taking "moral autonomy" as a central moral concept appears very close to Sartre and de Beauvoir's argument (p. 219). Warnock, *Existentialist Ethics*, p. 40, is aware of the argument; she says it contains "various doubtful steps," but does not elaborate.
22. *Praxis and Action*, pp. 154–155 n.
23. Ibid., pp. 151–154.
24. *For an Ontology of Morals*, pp. 76–77.
25. *Being and Nothingness*, p. 625.
26. Ibid, p. 628; *The Ethics of Ambiguity*, pp. 74–81.
27. Marcel, *The Philosophy of Existentialism*, trans. M. Harari

(New York: Citadel Press, 1962), p. 86. Unnamed Marxists are referred to by Sartre in "Materialism and Revolution," p. 244. Bernstein voices the same objection, *Praxis and Action*, p. 152, as does Jolivet, *Sartre: The Theology of the Absurd*, pp. 62–63.

28. *Being and Nothingness*, p. 550.
29. Ibid., p. 549.
30. Plantinga, "An Existentialist's Ethics," 248–250; Richard Beis, "Atheistic Existentialist Ethics: A Critique," *Modern Schoolman* 42 (1965): 168–169.
31. *The Ethics of Ambiguity*, p. 72.
32. *Being and Nothingness*, p. 625; Jeanson, *Le problème moral et la pensée de Sartre*, pp. 30–31, 289, makes the same point.
33. *Being and Nothingness*, pp. 479 and 510; *The Ethics of Ambiguity*, p. 40.
34. *The Ethics of Ambiguity*, p. 16; also see p. 32.
35. *Being and Nothingness*, pp. 482–485; *Existentialism and Humanism*, p. 52; "Materialism and Revolution," pp. 235–237. An excellent study of the various meanings of freedom in Sartre has been done by N. McLeod, "Existential Freedom in the Marxism of J.-P. Sartre," *Dialogue* 7 (1968–1969).
36. *Existentialism and Humanism*, p. 52. De Beauvoir is particularly good in explaining this, *The Ethics of Ambiguity*, pp. 24–34. Also see Jeanson, *Le problème moral et la pensée de Sartre*, pp. 27, 28, 239, 240.
37. See, for example, *Anti-Semite and Jew*, p. 148. Also *Search for a Method*, trans. Hazel Barnes (New York: Vintage Books, 1968), pp. 91–96, and "Introduction to Vol. I of *Les Temps Modernes*," in *Paths to the Present*, ed. E. Weber (New York: Dodd, Mead, 1960), p. 441.
38. Wild, "Authentic Existence: A New Approach to 'Value Theory,'" pp. 62–63; Olson, "Authenticity, Metaphysics, and Moral Responsibility," 106–107; Jolivet, *Sartre: The Theology of the Absurd*, pp. 65–67. Also see n. 54 below.
39. *Being and Nothingness*, p. 483. In fact, this work is almost totally concerned with freedom in the sense of the ontological structure of man and freedom of choice, saying very little about freedom of attaining.
40. Interview in *Oui*, 122; "The Itinerary of a Thought," interview published in *Between Existentialism and Marxism*, pp.

33–35; de Beauvoir, *Force of Circumstance*, p. 242; Jeanson, *Sartre dans sa vie*, pp. 265–267, 274.

41. "Materialism and Revolution," p. 244.
42. *What Is Literature?*, p. 43.
43. *Critique of Dialectical Reason*, p. 90; *Search for a Method*, pp. 91, 150–151, 171 n. What was called lack and desire in *Being and Nothingness* is apparently called need in the *Critique*.
44. *Existentialism and Humanism*, p. 46.
45. *Being and Nothingness*, p. 456; see also pp. 567–568.
46. See, for example, *Anti-Semite and Jew*, p. 60: "What men have in common is not a 'nature' but a condition, that is, an ensemble of limits and restrictions: the inevitability of death, the necessity of working for a living, of living in a world already inhabited by other men. Fundamentally this condition is nothing more than the basic human situation, or, if you prefer, the ensemble of abstract characteristics common to all situations. I agree therefore with the democrat that the Jew is a man like other men, but this tells me nothing in particular—except that he is free, that he is at the same time in bondage, that he is born, enjoys life, suffers, and dies, that he loves and hates, just as do all men. I can derive nothing more from these excessively general data." Also refer to "Introduction to Vol. I of *Les Temps Modernes*," p. 438, and *On a raison de se révolter*, p. 342. Jeanson does not hesitate to use the term "essence"; see *Le problème moral et la pensée de Sartre*, p. 257.
47. Jeanson, ibid., pp. 342–343. Sartre in *On a raison de se révolter*, pp. 345–352, emphasizes the connection between freedom and power. To be free is to have power, in this case power to fulfill needs. Olafson's criticism of Sartre and de Beauvoir, *Principles and Persons*, p. 206, for downgrading empirical desires, and Wild's similar criticism, "Authentic Existence: A New Approach to 'Value Theory,'" pp. 62–63, seem overstated in the light of Sartre's emphasis on need.
48. *The Ethics of Ambiguity*, pp. 79–81.
49. Ibid., p. 79.
50. *Being and Nothingness*, pp. 580–581. Note also that he states in these pages that a study of play properly belongs to ethics.
51. *Critique of Dialectical Reason*, p. 800.

52. "France: Masses, Spontaneity, Party," an interview in *Between Existentialism and Marxism*, pp. 124–125.
53. By using the terms "act" and "action" here I do not mean to imply that Sartre's is an act rather than a rule type of ethics. No indication is given as to which it is. On this point consult Olafson, *Principles and Persons*, chap. 7, sec. 4.
54. One prestigious ethician who labels it deontological is Frankena, *Ethics*, pp. 16, 23. I am using the terms "teleological" and "deontological" as he does.
55. Hazel Barnes, *An Existentialist Ethics* (Chicago: University of Chicago Press, 1978), chap. 1, especially pp. 23–26.
56. De Beauvoir, *Force of Circumstance*, p. 242; also see pp. 67–68, 261. Two close friends of theirs make the same point: Jeanson, *Sartre dans sa vie*, pp. 265–267; Andre Gorz, "Jean-Paul Sartre: From Consciousness to Praxis," trans. T. Busch in *Philosophy Today* 19 (Winter 1975): 289–291. Recently, Sartre has again described his evolution from individualism to an awareness of the social dimension of human existence. See "Self-Portrait at Seventy," pp. 44–48, 54.

CHAPTER 4

1. *Being and Nothingness*, p. 410. De Beauvoir in her early work *Pyrrhus et Cinéas* (Paris: Gallimard, 1944) says much the same, pp. 78–90.
2. Andre Gorz, "Jean-Paul Sartre: From Consciousness to Praxis," offers this interpretation, 289.
3. *Force of Circumstance*, p. 242; interview in *Oui*, 126.
4. *Force of Circumstance*, pp. 243, 261. For a discussion of this point, see Joseph McMahon, *Humans Being* (Chicago: University of Chicago Press, 1971), chap. 9.
5. *Existentialism and Humanism*, p. 52. (I translate "liberté" here as "freedom.")
6. Countless authors have maintained that according to Sartre's ontology all human relations are relations of conflict. Some examples are: Grene, *Sartre*, p. 253; George Stack, *Sartre's Philosophy of Social Existence* (St. Louis: Warren H. Green, Inc., 1977), pp. 113–114; Desan, *The Tragic Finale*, chap. 4; James Collins, *The Existentialists* (Chicago: Regnery Co., 1963), p. 84; Hartmann, *Sartre's Ontology*, chap. 5; Warnock,

Existentialist Ethics, pp. 45–50. Sartre himself in *Critique of Dialectical Reason,* pp. 227–228 n., apparently admits that *Being and Nothingness* is open to this interpretation.

7. *Being and Nothingness,* p. 364.
8. Ibid., p. 429.
9. *Sartre's Philosophy of Social Existence,* p. 114.
10. *Existentialist Ethics,* p. 47.
11. *Being and Nothingness,* p. 244.
12. Ibid., p. 247.
13. Ibid., p. 283.
14. Ibid., p. 284.
15. Ibid., pp. 364 and 428.
16. "Self-Portrait at Seventy," p. 9. See also "The Writer and His Language," interview with Pierre Verstraeten in *Politics and Literature,* trans. J. A. Underwood and John Calder (London: Calder and Boyars, 1973), p. 96.
17. *Being and Nothingness,* pp. 413, 414.
18. Ibid., pp. 252–272.
19. Ibid., p. 410.
20. Ibid., pp. 408–410.
21. Ibid., p. 364; also see p. 428.
22. Ibid., pp. 362–363. McMahon, *Humans Being,* is one of the very few commentators who show awareness of this context, pp. 248–256.
23. *Being and Nothingness,* p. 412. One critic who finds this footnote impossible to understand is M. Warnock, *The Philosophy of Sartre,* p. 130. One should recall that Sartre later referred to *Being and Nothingness* as a description of men in bad faith. See n. 31 of chap. 2.
24. See above, chap. 2, sec. B, pp. 27–34. Jeanson, *Le problème moral et la pensée de Sartre,* interprets the radical conversion in this way and goes on to say that conflict with others will lose its meaning once men cease trying to be God, pp. 224–227. De Beauvoir identifies this conversion with the "Husserlian reduction," *The Ethics of Ambiguity,* p. 14. For a good discussion of this, see the article by Thomas Busch, "Sartre: The Phenomenological Reduction and Human Relationships," *Journal of the British Society for Phenomenology* 6 (January 1975).
25. *Being and Nothingness,* p. 526; also see p. 410. The same point is made in *Critique of Dialectical Reason,* p. 105.

26. *Being and Nothingness,* pt. 4, chap. 1, sec. 3.
27. *Existentialism and Humanism,* p. 29.
28. Ibid., p. 30. A similar claim is made in "Introduction to Vol. I of *Les Temps Modernes,*" p. 441.
29. *Existentialist Ethics,* p. 41.
30. I believe the contemporary British philosopher R. M. Hare makes the same assumption by claiming that it is analytically true that reasons given in support of a moral choice involve universal maxims, "Universalisability," *Proceedings of the Aristotelian Society* 55 (1954–1955).
31. *Praxis and Action,* p. 153.
32. *Existentialism and Humanism,* pp. 51–52 (my translation in part). A similar statement is made in *What Is Literature?,* p. 41.
33. *Existentialism and Humanism,* p. 45.
34. *Being and Nothingness,* p. 262.
35. Ibid., pp. 275, 524–531.
36. Ibid., p. 275.
37. *Saint Genet,* pp. 41–44; *Search for a Method,* pp. 60–65; "On The Idiot of the Family," pp. 117–118; "Elections: A Trap for Fools," published in *Life/Situations,* pp. 200–202, 207. His discussion of extero-conditioning (other-direction) in *Critique* is most instructive on this point, bk. 2, chap. 6, sec. 6.
38. *Saint Genet,* p. 46.
39. *Anti-Semite and Jew,* p. 151. A similar suggestion seems to be presented in "Vietnam: Imperialism and Genocide," in *Between Existentialism and Marxism,* p. 83.
40. *Anti-Semite and Jew,* p. 153.
41. *Critique of Dialectical Reason,* p. 111.
42. A. Manser, *Sartre: A Philosophic Study,* pp. 157–158, and H. Barnes, *An Existentialist Ethics,* pp. 61–62, suggest this argument for Sartre. I offered this also in my article "Is a Sartrean Ethics Possible?" in *Philosophy Today* 14 (1970): 126–130. I have since changed my mind about its validity.
43. Marjorie Grene obliquely refers to it in a footnote in *Introduction to Existentialism* (Chicago: University of Chicago, Phoenix Books, 1958), p. 120. Olafson, *Principles and Persons,* chap. 8, sec. 4, offers an argument similar in many respects to de Beauvoir's, though he makes no explicit reference to hers. Jeanson, "Les caractères existentialistes de la

conduite humaine selon Jean-Paul Sartre," p. 192, has a hint of the same argument.
44. *The Ethics of Ambiguity*, p. 72; see also *Pyrrhus et Cinéas*, pp. 95–96.
45. *Pyrrhus et Cinéas*, pp. 99–101, 116–117.
46. Ibid., pp. 114–115. All translations from this work are my own.
47. Ibid., p. 115.
48. Ibid., p. 116.
49. Ibid., p. 112.
50. Ibid.
51. Ibid., p. 116.
52. *The Ethics of Ambiguity*, p. 135.
53. In *The Ethics of Ambiguity*, pp. 100–115, she shows she is aware of the difficulty.

CHAPTER 5

1. *Critique of Dialectical Reason*, pp. 436–437.
2. Ibid., p. 673.
3. Warnock, *The Philosophy of Sartre*, p. 175.
4. *Existentialist Ethics*, p. 52.
5. *Sartre's Philosophy of Social Existence*, pp. 123–124.
6. Ibid., p. 128. Chiodi, *Sartre and Marxism*, trans. K. Soper (Atlantic Highlands: Humanities Press, 1976), pp. 93–99, says the same.
7. *Sartre's Philosophy of Social Existence*, p. 128; Warnock, *The Philosophy of Sartre*, p. 180; Grene, *Sartre*, pp. 219–222.
8. *Being and Nothingness*, pt. 3, chap. 3, sec. 3B.
9. Ibid., pp. 424, 425, 428, 429.
10. *Critique of Dialectical Reason*, bk. 1, chap. 3, sec. 1.
11. Ibid., pp. 226–228, 336–337, 369–370 passim.
12. "France: Masses, Spontaneity, Party," pp. 124–125.
13. See his discussion of the series, *Critique of Dialectical Reason*, bk. 1, chap. 4, sec. 1.
14. Ibid., pp. 123–125, 804; *Search for a Method*, p. 34; "Self-Portrait at Seventy," 13; "Je ne suis plus réaliste," an interview with Pierre Verstraeten in *Gulliver*, no. 1 (November 1972): 42.
15. *Critique of Dialectical Reason*, pp. 672–673.

16. Ibid., pp. 106–109. What exactly "actualization" means, however, is unclear. Does the third party simply make manifest a unity already present or does he provide this unity? In bk. 1, chap. 2, sec. 2, texts can be found to support either interpretation. For an excellent discussion of the role of the third in the group, consult the article by Thomas Flynn, "The Alienating and the Mediating Third in the Social Philosophy of Jean-Paul Sartre," *Studies in Philosophy and the History of Philosophy*, vol. 6 (1973), ed. John K. Ryan (Washington, D.C.: Catholic University of America Press).

17. *Critique of Dialectical Reason*, pp. 389, 391, 401.

18. Ibid., p. 390–402.

19. Ibid., p. 668.

20. Ibid., p. 373.

21. Ibid., p. 377; see also p. 373.

22. Ibid., pp. 392, 402.

23. Ibid., pp. 394–395.

24. Ibid., pp. 378, 386–387, 393–394, 400, 403.

25. Ibid., pp. 394, 402–403.

26. Ibid., p. 424; see also pp. 379–381, 396–398.

27. Ibid., pp. 176, 810.

28. Ibid., p. 378.

29. Ibid., pp. 110–115. De Beauvoir, too, in various places, speaks of treating others as *both* subjects and objects at the same time: *The Ethics of Ambiguity*, p. 67; *The Second Sex*, trans. and ed. H. M. Parshley (New York: Vintage Books, 1952), pp. 158, 741. Warnock, *Existentialist Ethics*, p. 47, claims that in *Critique* Sartre asserts that we can never adopt other people as ends in themselves. This is simply incorrect. What he says is we can never treat others (or even ourselves) as "absolute ends." We will also always deal with them (and with ourselves) as means, *Critique of Dialectical Reason*, p. 112.

30. *Critique of Dialectical Reason*, pp. 436–437.

31. Ibid., pp. 419–425, 436.

32. Ibid., pp. 418, 440.

33. Ibid., p. 422.

34. Ibid., pp. 424, 435.

35. Ibid., p. 437; also see pp. 581–583. Chap. 4 of pt. 2 is an extensive discussion of the ontological reality of the group.

As far as I can see, it does not solve the basic problem of the precise nature of the group's reality.
36. Ibid., p. 437.
37. Ibid., pp. 402, 424.
38. Ibid., pp. 423–425. It is interesting to note that on p. 423 Sartre does use the expression "quasi-object" of the pledged group, but in the pages immediately following he drops the "quasi."
39. Ibid., p. 434.
40. Ibid.
41. Ibid., pp. 424–426.
42. Ibid., p. 437.
43. Ibid., p. 679; see, in general, pp. 671–678.
44. Wilfrid Desan, *The Marxism of Sartre* (Garden City: Doubleday Anchor Books, 1966), p. 175; "France: Masses, Spontaneity, Party," pp. 122–123.
45. "The Itinerary of a Thought," pp. 57–58; "France: Masses, Spontaneity, Party," pp. 131–133; *On a raison de se révolter*, pp. 46–48.
46. *Critique of Dialectical Reason*, bk. 1, chap. 3, sec. 3.
47. Ibid., p. 226.
48. Ibid., p. 227.
49. Ibid., p. 672.
50. Ibid., p. 673.
51. Ibid.
52. Ibid., pp. 434, 436.
53. Ibid., pp. 378, 411. Bk. 2, chap. 4, sec. 1 discusses the intelligibility of the group.
54. Flynn, "The Alienating and the Mediating Third in the Social Philosophy of Jean-Paul Sartre," p. 32. Sartre uses the phrase "dialectical nominalism" in *Critique of Dialectical Reason*, p. 37.
55. Stack, *Sartre's Philosophy of Social Existence*, p. 124.
56. *On a raison de se révolter*, pp. 77, 185–186.
57. "Self-Portrait at Seventy," pp. 11–13, 62–63, 69.
58. "The Maoists in France," pp. 167–168, and "Elections: A Trap for Fools," pp. 201–202, essays in *Life/Situations*.
59. See chap. 2, n. 32.
60. Recall that I mentioned earlier that Sartre told de Beauvoir about the tension he felt between the requirements of per-

sonal freedom on the one hand and the need for community on the other. See chap. 4, n. 4.

61. *Critique of Dialectical Reason,* n. 89 on pp. 306–307.
62. "Self-Portrait at Seventy," p. 13.
63. I have often disagreed with Warnock's interpretation of Sartre. But on this point—the Hobbesian character of Sartre's view of man—I am in complete agreement with what she says in *The Philosophy of Sartre,* pp. 173–175.

CHAPTER 6

1. Michel-Antoine Burnier, *Choice of Action,* trans. Bernard Murchland (New York: Random House, 1968); Mark Poster, *Existentialist Marxism in Postwar France* (Princeton: Princeton University Press, 1975); Jeanson, *Sartre dans sa vie.*
2. ". . . Said Jean-Paul Sartre," an interview with Henri Magnan in *Yale French Studies* 16 (Winter 1955–1956): 5. His abortive attempt to set up a political organization, the Rassemblement Démocratique Révolutionnaire, is described by Burnier in *Choice of Action,* chap. 4.
3. *Search for a Method,* p. 34; *What Is Literature?,* p. 108; *On a raison de se révolter,* pp. 258–259, 337–340.
4. *Critique of Dialectical Reason,* p. 661.
5. *On a raison de se révolter,* p. 307. All translations from this work are my own. See also *Critique of Dialectical Reason,* pp. 654–655 n. 88.
6. *On a raison de se révolter,* p. 108; *Anti-Semite and Jew,* pp. 149-150; interview in *Esquire,* 208; Poster, *Existential Marxism in Postwar France,* p. 296.
7. *On a raison de se révolter,* pp. 300–303. "Self-Portrait at Seventy," p. 63.
8. "Self-Portrait at Seventy," p. 13.
9. "Revolution and the Intellectual," an interview with Jean-Claude Garot in *Politics and Literature,* pp. 18, 19; *On a raison de se révolter,* pp. 300–305.
10. Interview in *Esquire,* 208; Jeanson, *Sartre dans sa vie,* p. 253.
11. *On a raison de se révolter,* pp. 47–48; *What Is Literature?,* pp. 107–108; "Self-Portrait at Seventy," pp. 24–25.
12. *On a raison de se révolter,* pp. 102, 300–305. See also "The Maoists in France," p. 167.

13. Marx's *German Ideology* as found in Erich Fromm, *Marx's Concept of Man* (New York: Frederick Ungar Publishing Co., 1961), p. 206.
14. *Critique of Dialectical Reason*, p. 800.
15. *On a raison de se révolter*, pp. 71, 325; "The Itinerary of a Thought," pp. 62–63.
16. "Self-Portrait at Seventy," p. 84; *On a raison de se révolter*, pp. 345–352.
17. In *Existentialism and Humanism*, pp. 42, 53, Sartre is very clear: "What counts is the total commitment, and it is not by a particular case or particular action that you are committed altogether."
18. "A Long, Bitter, Sweet Madness," 62.
19. Manser, *Sartre: A Philosophic Study*, pp. 167–168. A similar criticism is voiced by Barnes, *An Existentialist Ethics*, pp. 34–35, 43–44.
20. Beis in his article "Atheist Existentialist Ethics: A Critique" compiled a list of the kinds of behavior approved and condemned by Sartre and de Beauvoir, 168–171. See also "Self-Portrait at Seventy," pp. 11–13, 63, and the interview in *Oui*, 123–124.
21. Philip Thody, *Jean-Paul Sartre: A Literary and Political Study* (London: Hamish Hamilton, 1960), pp. 218–223. De Beauvoir was more hesitant, *The Ethics of Ambiguity*, pp. 146–147.
22. *What Is Literature?*, p. 200; "The Itinerary of a Thought," pp. 58–59.
23. Interview in *Oui*, 122, 123.
24. *What Is Literature?*, p. 199; de Beauvoir, *The Ethics of Ambiguity*, p. 124.
25. "The Ghost of Stalin," *Les Temps Modernes*, no. 131 (1957): 674, as quoted by Manser, *Sartre: A Philosophic Study*, p. 195.
26. *What Is Literature?*, p. 199.
27. "Capitulation ou contre-escalade," *Les Temps Modernes*, no. 243 (1966): 193–196; interview in *Oui*, 123, 124.
28. *The Ethics of Ambiguity*, chap. 3, secs. 3, 4, 5.
29. Ibid., p. 114.
30. *What Is Literature?*, p. 199; *The Ethics of Ambiguity*, pp. 113–115.
31. *The Ethics of Ambiguity*, p. 134.

32. Barnes, *Sartre*, p. 187.
33. John Stuart Mill, *Utilitarianism*, ed. Oskar Piest, The Library of Liberal Arts (New York: Bobbs-Merrill Company, Inc., 1957), chap. 4.
34. *On a raison de se révolter*, p. 45; "The Maoists in France," p. 170. See also "A Plea for Intellectuals," p. 256; "A Friend of the People," p. 292.
35. *Being and Nothingness*, p. 90.
36. *The Ethics of Ambiguity*, pp. 157–158.
37. Raymond Aron makes this point as quoted by Poster, *Existential Marxism in Postwar France*, p. 192.
38. "A Long, Bitter, Sweet Madness," p. 61.
39. R. Linton, "Universal Ethical Principles: An Anthropological Approach," in *Moral Principles of Action*, ed. R. N. Anshem (New York: Harper and Row, 1952); C. Kluckhohn, "Ethical Relativity, Sic et Non," *Journal of Philosophy* 52 (1955): 663–667; R. Redfield, "The Universally Human and the Culturally Variable," *The Journal of General Education* 10 (July 1967): 150–160.

Bibliography

This bibliography contains the works I have referred to in this book. A complete, annotated bibliography of all of Sartre's writings through 1973 is available in volume 1 of the work by M. Contat and M. Rybalka cited below. Two very extensive international bibliographies of secondary literature on Sartre are the following: F. and C. Lapointe, *Jean-Paul Sartre and His Critics: An International Bibliography (1938–1975)* (Bowling Green, Ohio: Philosophy Documentation Center, 1975); R. Wilcocks, *Jean-Paul Sartre: A Bibliography of International Criticism* (Edmonton, Canada: The University of Alberta Press, 1975). The latter also contains a bibliography of bibliographies.

PRIMARY SOURCES

De Beauvoir, Simone:

The Ethics of Ambiguity. Trans. Bernard Frechtman. New York: Citadel Press, 1967.
Force of Circumstance. Trans. Richard Howard. New York: G. P. Putnam's Sons, 1964.
Pyrrhus et Cinéas. Paris: Gallimard, 1944.
The Second Sex. Trans. and ed. H. M. Parshley. New York: Vintage Books, 1974.

Bibliography

Sartre, Jean-Paul:

Anti-Semite and Jew. Trans. G. Becker. New York: Schocken
Books, 1948.

Being and Nothingness. Trans. Hazel E. Barnes. New York:
Philosophical Library, 1956.

Between Existentialism and Marxism. Trans. John Matthews.
London: NLB, 1974. (Among the contents of this book are
the following pieces cited in my footnotes: "The Purpose of
Writing," "The Itinerary of a Thought," "Vietnam: Im-
perialism and Genocide," "France: Masses, Spontaneity,
Party," "A Plea for Intellectuals," and "A Friend of the
People."

"Capitulation ou contre-escalade," *Les Temps Modernes,* no. 243
(August 1966): 193–196.

"Consciousness of Self and Knowledge of Self." In *Readings in
Existential Phenomenology,* pp. 113–142. Ed. N. Lawrence
and D. O'Connor. Trans. Mary Ellen and N. Lawrence.
Englewood Cliffs, N.J.: Prentice-Hall, Inc., 1967.

"Conversation with Jean-Paul Sartre." Interview in *Oui* 4 (June
1975): 69–70, 122–126.

Critique of Dialectical Reason. Trans. Alan Sheridan-Smith.
London: NLB, 1976.

"Determinism and Freedom." In *The Writings of Jean-Paul
Sartre.* Vol. II, pp. 241–252. Ed. M. Contat and M. Rybalka.
Trans. R. McCleary. Evanston, Ill.: Northwestern Univer-
sity Press, 1974.

Existentialism and Humanism. Trans. P. Mairet. London: Eyre
Methuen Ltd., 1973.

"In gesprek met Jean-Paul Sartre." Interview by C. Van Peursen
in *Wending* (The Hague) 9 (March 1954): 15–24.

"Introduction to Vol. 1 of *Les Temps Modernes.*" In *Paths to the
Present,* pp. 432–441. Ed. E. Weber. New York: Dodd,
Mead, 1960.

"Je ne suis plus réaliste." Interview by P. Vertraeten in *Gulliver,*
no. 1 (November 1972): 39–46.

Life/Situations. Trans. P. Auster and L. Davis. New York:
Pantheon Books, 1977. (Among the contents of this book are
the following pieces cited in my footnotes: "Self-Portrait at
Seventy," "On *The Idiot of the Family,*" "The Maoists in
France," "Elections: A Trap for Fools.")

"A Long, Bitter, Sweet Madness." Interview with *Le Monde.*

Trans. Anthony Hartley and published in *Encounter* 22, no. 6 (June 1964): 61–63.

"Materialism and Revolution." In *Literary and Philosophical Essays*, pp. 198–256. Trans. Annette Michelson. New York: Collier Books, 1962.

On a raison de se révolter. A collection of interviews with Ph. Gavi and P. Victor. Paris: Gallimard, 1974.

Politics and Literature. Trans. J. A. Underwood and J. Calder. London: Calder and Boyars, 1973. (Among the contents of this book are the following pieces cited in my footnotes: "Revolution and the Intellectual" and "The Writer and His Language.")

". . . Said Jean-Paul Sartre." Interview with Henri Magnan in *Yale French Studies* 16 (Winter 1955–1956): 3–7.

Saint Genet: Actor and Martyr. Trans. B. Frechtman. New York: New American Library, Mentor Books, 1963.

"Sartre Accuses the Intellectuals of Bad Faith." Interview with John Gerassi in *New York Times Magazine*, October 17, 1971, pp. 38–39, 116–119.

Search for a Method. Trans. Hazel Barnes. New York: Vintage Books, 1968.

Situations, IV. Paris: Gallimard, 1964.

The Transcendence of the Ego. Trans. F. Williams and R. Kirkpatrick. New York: The Noonday Press, Inc., 1957.

"We Write for Our Own Time." Trans. Sylvia Glass. *Virginia Quarterly Review* 23 (April 1947): 236–243.

What Is Literature? Trans. B. Frechtman. New York: Washington Square Press, Inc., 1966.

"What's Jean-Paul Sartre Thinking Lately?" Interview by P. Bénichou in *Esquire* 78 (December 1972): 204–208, 280–286.

The Words. Trans. B. Frechtman. Greenwich, Conn.: Fawcett Publications, Inc., 1966.

SECONDARY SOURCES

Anderson, Thomas C. "Neglected Sartrean Arguments for the Freedom of Consciousness." *Philosophy Today* 17 (Spring 1973): 28–39.

———. "Is a Sartrean Ethics Possible?" *Philosophy Today* 14 (Summer 1970): 116–140.

Barnes, Hazel. *An Existentialist Ethics.* Chicago: University of Chicago Press, 1978.

————. *Sartre.* New York: J. B. Lippincott Co., 1973.

Beis, Richard. "Atheist Existentialist Ethics: A Critique." *Modern Schoolman* 42 (January 1965): 153–177.

Bernstein, Richard. *Praxis and Action.* Philadelphia: University of Pennsylvania Press, 1971.

Burnier, Michel-Antoine. *Choice of Action.* Trans. B. Murchland. New York: Random House, 1968.

Busch, Thomas. "Sartre: The Phenomenological Reduction and Human Relationships." *Journal of the British Society for Phenomenology* 6 (January 1975): 55–61.

Chiodi, Pietro. *Sartre and Marxism.* Trans. Kate Soper. Atlantic Highlands, N.J.: Humanities Press, 1976.

Collins, James. *The Existentialists.* Chicago: Henry Regnery Co., 1963.

Contat, Michel, and Rybalka, Michel. *The Writings of Jean-Paul Sartre.* Vol. 1. Trans. R. McCleary. Evanston, Ill.: Northwestern University Press, 1974.

Danto, Arthur. *Jean-Paul Sartre.* New York: The Viking Press, 1975.

Desan, Wilfrid. *The Tragic Finale.* New York: Harper and Row, 1960.

————. *The Marxism of Jean-Paul Sartre.* Garden City, N.Y.: Doubleday and Co., Inc., 1966.

Flynn, Thomas. "The Alienating and the Mediating Third in the Social Philosophy of Jean-Paul Sartre." In *Studies in Philosophy and the History of Philosophy,* vol. 6, pp. 3–38. Ed. John Ryan. Washington, D.C.: Catholic University of America Press, 1973.

Frankena, William. *Ethics.* 2d ed. Englewood Cliffs, N.J.: Prentice-Hall, Inc., 1973.

Frankl, Viktor. *The Doctor and The Soul.* New York: Random House, Inc., 1963.

————. *Man's Search for Meaning.* New York: Simon & Schuster, Inc., 1963.

Fromm, Erich. *Marx's Concept of Man.* New York: Frederick Ungar Publishing Co., 1964.

Gorz, Andre. "Jean-Paul Sartre: From Consciousness to Praxis." Trans. T. Busch. *Philosophy Today* 19 (Winter 1975): 283–286.

Grene, Marjorie. *Sartre.* New York: New Viewpoints, 1973.
––––––. *Introduction to Existentialism.* Chicago: University of Chicago Press, 1963.
––––––. "Authenticity: An Existentialist Virtue." *Ethics* 62 (July 1952): 266–274.
Hare, R. M. "Universalisability." *Proceedings of the Aristotelian Society* 55 (1954–1955): 295–312.
Hartmann, Klaus. *Sartre's Ontology.* Evanston, Ill.: Northwestern University Press, 1966.
Hudson, W. D. *Modern Moral Philosophy.* Garden City: Doubleday and Co., Inc., 1970.
Jeanson, Francis. *Sartre dans sa vie.* Paris: Éditions du Seuil, 1974.
––––––. *Le problème moral et la pensée de Sartre.* Paris: Éditions du Seuil, 1965.
––––––. "Les caractères existentialistes de la conduite humaine selon Jean-Paul Sartre." In *Morale Chrétienne et Requêtes Contemporaines,* by F.-M. Braun et al. Paris: Casterman, 1954.
Jolivet, Régis. *Sartre: The Theology of the Absurd.* Trans. W. Piersol. New York: Newman Press, 1967.
Kluckhohn, Clyde. "Ethical Relativity, Sic et Non." *Journal of Philosophy* 52 (1955): 663–667.
Linton, Ralph. "Universal Ethical Principles: An Anthropological Approach." In *Moral Principles of Action.* Ed. R. N. Anshem. New York: Harper and Row, 1952.
Manser, Anthony. *Sartre, A Philosophic Study.* New York: Oxford University Press, 1967.
Marcel, Gabriel. *The Philosophy of Existentialism.* Trans. Manya Harari. New York: The Citadel Press, 1962.
McLeod, Norman. "Existential Freedom in the Marxism of Jean-Paul Sartre." *Dialogue* 7 (June 1968): 26–44.
McMahon, Joseph. *Humans Being: The World of Jean-Paul Sartre.* Chicago: University of Chicago Press, 1971.
Mill, John Stuart. *Utilitarianism.* Ed. Oskar Piest. The Library of Liberal Arts. New York: Bobbs-Merrill Co., Inc., 1957.
Nietzsche, Friedrich. *Thus Spoke Zarathustra.* Trans. R. J. Hollingdale. New York: Penguin Books, 1969.
Olafson, Frederick. *Principles and Persons.* Baltimore: Johns Hopkins Press, 1970.

Olson, Robert. "Authenticity, Metaphysics, and Moral Responsibility." *Philosophy* 34 (1959): 99–110.

Plantinga, Alvin. "An Existentialist's Ethics." *Review of Meta-Physics* 12 (December 1958): 235–256.

Poster, Mark. *Existential Marxism in Postwar France.* Princeton, N.J.: Princeton University Press, 1975.

Redfield, R. "The Universally Human and the Culturally Variable." *The Journal of General Education* 10 (July 1967): 150–160.

Scheler, Max. *Formalism in Ethics and Non-Formal Ethics of Values.* Trans. Manfred Frings and Roger Funk. Evanston, Ill.: Northwestern University Press, 1973.

Stack, George. *Sartre's Philosophy of Social Existence.* St. Louis: Warren H. Green, Inc., 1977.

Thody, Philip. *Jean-Paul Sartre: A Literary and Political Study.* London: Hamish Hamilton, 1960.

Veatch, Henry. *For an Ontology of Morals.* Evanston, Ill.: Northwestern University Press, 1971.

Warnock, Geoffrey. *Contemporary Moral Philosophy.* New York: St. Martin's Press, Inc., 1967.

Warnock, Mary. *The Philosophy of Sartre.* New York: Barnes and Noble, Inc., 1967.

———. *Existentialist Ethics.* London: Macmillan, 1967.

Wild, John. "Authentic Existence: A New Approach to 'Value Theory'." In *An Invitation to Phenomenology,* pp. 59–77. Ed. James Edie. Chicago: Quadrangle Books, Inc., 1965.

Index

absurd, absurdity, 135, 148
action(s): common, in the group, 98, 100–106, 109, 110, 116, 118, 119, 130; freedom of, 53, 55 (*see also* freedom, to attain goals); and the intellectual, 8, 11; morality of, 60, 61, 65, 130, 140, 160 n.53, 167 nn.17, 20; regulated by others, 105, 106, 116, 117; unity of (*see* unity, of common action). *See also* acts; conduct
acts: as attempts to be God, 16–19, 26, 27, 29, 31; create an image of man, 79, 81; morality of, 60, 61, 130–132, 160 n.53. *See also* action(s), conduct
Algiers, 131, 132
alienation, 126, 148; acceptance of, 77; attempts to overcome, 74–76, 102, 103, 115, 118; of conscious subjects, 72–76, 106; in contemporary industrial society, 102, 129, 130; as domination by external forces, 102, 103, 106, 115, 121, 129; of freedom, 68, 73, 75, 77, 108, 132; and the group, 102–104, 106, 115, 121; and scarcity, 101, 102, 123; total elimination

of, 103, 104, 123. *See also* objectification, as alienation; reification, as alienation
anarchist, Sartre as, 128
Anti-Semite and Jew, 43, 85, 93
Aristotle (Aristotelianism), 123, 124, 140
atheism, 3, 20, 22
atomism, overcome by group, 104, 105, 119
atoms, men as isolated, 102, 104, 119
authenticity: as abstraction, 44, 61; as choice of freedom, 44, 45, 53, 61, 67, 110, 147, 148; definition of, 43, 44, 61; as good faith, 43, 45; and a meaningful life, 147, 148

Baader-Meinhoff gang, 135
bad faith, 16, 38, 61, 146; *Being and Nothingness* as description of men in, 32, 121, 161 n.23; choice of, 44, 46, 49, 53; as denial of freedom, 41, 83, 93; and the spirit of seriousness, 20, 21, 30, 67
Barnes, Hazel, 64, 138
Being and Nothingness, 4, 6, 12, 13,

175

human relations," 98, 115, 116, 118; as the ideal human relationship, 97–99, 103, 107, 116; the masses and, 127, 142; ontological status of, 103, 104, 113, 115–117, 120, 164 n.35; power of, 99, 102, 103, 105, 107; prefigured in we-subject, 100, 101; relation of individual to (*see* individual, and the group); remaining in its initial stage, 113–115, 118, 128, 129; restriction and limitation of freedom in, 98, 99, 103, 105, 106, 108, 113, 114; union of men in, 97, 103–107, 113, 116–118. *See also* group, pledged

group, pledged: enhancement of freedom in, 110, 112, 115–117; as the ideal human relationship, 108, 110, 115, 116, 118, 119; as its own object, 110–113, 115, 116, 165 n.38; nature and purpose of, 108–113, 116, 118, 119; restriction and limitation of freedom in, 110–113, 116; superior to spontaneous group, 108, 109, 116; union of men in, 109–112, 116, 117, 119, 120, 122. *See also* brothers, men as; obligation, formal

group, spontaneous (also called group in fusion), 98, 101, 108–114, 116, 121, 123. *See also* group, the (in general)

guilt, 73

Hare, R. M., 155 n.36, 162 n.30
hate, 73, 74, 76
Hegel, G. W. F., 70
Heidegger, Martin, 69, 70
"Hell is other people," 69
Hitler, Adolf, 146, 147
Hobbes, Thomas (Hobbesian), 123, 143, 166 n.63
hostility. *See* conflict, as actual hostility
humanism, 59, 140, 141
humanity, group as origin of, 98, 108, 109

Hungarian Freedom Fighters, 135

I-Thou relation, 124
identity (identification) with others, 105, 111, 117, 121. *See also* same, the
L'Idiot de la Famille, 7
individual, the, 9, 10, 80; always ontologically separate from others, 70–72, 75, 76, 104, 109, 116, 120, 123; common, 99, 109; as expendable, 113, 119; and the group, 98–101, 103–105, 109–111, 113, 116, 117, 119, 120; and human needs, 57–59; no individual salvation possible for, 65, 67, 68, 132, 140; in we-subject relation, 100, 101. *See also* separateness, ontological
individual, the authentic, 60, 122. *See also* authenticity
individualism, Sartre's, 9, 10, 65, 67, 68, 91, 120, 122, 123, 140, 143, 152 n.10, 160 n.56
inertia and the group, 98, 108, 112
institution, the, 99, 108, 128, 134, 142; evolution of the group to, 99, 108, 113, 115, 118
intellectual, the: role of, 8–12, 126, 138, 142, 143; worker, 129
interdependence of men's freedoms, 82–87, 89, 94, 110, 123. *See also* other, the: dependency on
is/ought distinction, 48. *See* facts

Jeanson, Francis, 4, 5, 13, 56, 152 n.10, 155 n.22, 156 n.2, 159 n.46, 161 n.24
Jew, the, 43, 85, 159 n.46
justification, 3; dependent on others, 86–90; and freedom, 18, 42, 46, 47, 50, 52, 53, 87–89, 145; from oneself, 18, 19, 26, 47, 122; of God's existence, 17, 18, 47, 87; of human existence, 17, 18, 42, 46, 47, 50–53, 64, 86–90, 122, 126; man's desire for, 17, 18, 38, 42,

46, 47, 50–52, 86–89, 122; maximum attainable, 47, 88–90, 126. *See also* meaning

Kantian morality, 79, 90
King, Martin Luther, Jr., 147
knowledge: and freedom of choice, 54–56; the other and one's self-, 83-85, 87, 89, 162 n.37; as reification of a subject, 92

lack: and desire, 19, 20, 24, 25, 29, 38, 39, 159 n.43; as freedom, 25, 31; man as, 19, 20, 24, 25, 29, 31, 38; and value, 23–25, 29–31
Levinas, Emmanuel, 92
liberation of men, 9, 55–57, 84, 132; the group and, 112, 116; violence and the, 135, 136
logic, 51, 52, 64, 135, 145, 148. *See also* consistency, logical
love, 92, 127, 133, 143, 144, 147; involving conflict, 69, 73, 74, 76; not reducible to common action, 119, 120, 123; rooted in the pledge, 110, 119
lying, 22, 133, 135, 137

man: as doomed to failure, 16, 20, 27, 28, 33–35, 77, 140; ontological structure of, 19, 20, 25, 29, 30–32, 38, 53, 54, 57, 58; as "useless passion," 15–20, 77, 78, 122, 148. For more information see specific items pertaining to man; such as: choice, desire to be God, desire for meaning, freedom, etc.
Maoists, French, 9
Marcel, Gabriel, 49, 92, 124
Marx, Karl, 102, 125–127, 129
Marxism, Sartre's alleged conversion to, 6, 76, 130
Marxists, 49, 55, 56, 94, 99, 127
masses, the, 11, 128; as alienated, 84, 102, 126, 127, 129; the goal of,

126, 142, 143; and the role of the intellectual, 8, 9, 11, 12, 126, 142, 143
"Materialism and Revolution," 42, 152 n.10
meaning: attainable by man, 33–35, 44, 51, 52, 139, 140, 147, 148; consistency and (*see* consistency, and a meaningful life); desire for, 17, 18, 38, 46, 47, 50–52, 63, 86–88, 90, 91, 94, 95, 122, 156 n.39; given by others, 38, 83, 84, 86–89, 92, 94, 123, 140, 145–147; of human existence (life), 3, 17, 18, 33–35, 38, 44, 46, 47, 50–53, 63–65, 87–90, 92, 94, 139, 143, 145–148; man as source of, 3, 18, 30, 33, 35, 46, 47, 52, 78, 86–88, 94, 139, 147, 148; of one's existence given by oneself, 18, 33, 38, 46, 47, 52, 81, 86, 87, 91, 92, 143, 145; as Sartre's primary goal, 146; value of, 50–53, 63, 64, 145, 146. *See also* consistency, and a meaningful life; justification; value
Mill, John Stuart, 141
mitsein, 69, 71
monism, ontological, 71, 120
Moore, G. E., 37
morality, 130; Kantian, 79, 90; of masses, 142, 143; same as ethics, 4, 42. *See also* ethics (in general); ethics, Sartre's
multiplicity, 105. *See* plurality
The Myth of Sisyphus, 148, 149

naturalistic fallacy, 34, 51, 63, 141
Nausea, 148
necessity: and God's existence, 16, 17; in the group's evolution, 99, 114, 115, 118; kinds of, 114; man's desire for, 17–20, 24–26, 29, 38, 74, 115, 148; man's lack of, 17–20, 25, 29–31, 38, 74; opposite of contingency and chance, 17–19, 25, 31
need(s), 159 n.43; common human,